PSALMS: A COMPANION VOLUME

PSALMS
A Companion Volume

Rabbi Hayyim Angel

KODESH PRESS

PSALMS: A COMPANION VOLUME
© Hayyim Angel 2022

Hardcover ISBN: 978-1-947857-85-8
Paperback ISBN: 978-1-947857-84-1

All rights reserved. Except for brief quotations in printed reviews, no part of this publication may be reproduced, stored in a retrieval system, or transmitted in any form or by any means (printed, written, photocopied, visual electronic, audio, or otherwise) without the prior permission of the publisher.

The publisher extends its gratitude to
Rabbi Eliezer Barany for editing this volume.

PUBLISHED AND DISTRIBUTED EXCLUSIVELY BY
Kodesh Press LLC
New York, NY
www.kodeshpress.com
kodeshpress@gmail.com

Set in Arno Pro and Ideal Sans
by Raphaël Freeman MISTD, Renana Typesetting

Printed in the United States of America

I thank my dear friends for their generous support
of the Institute for Jewish Ideas and Ideals

*Bengualid Family Foundation, in
memory of Sylvia Knafou Bengualid*

*Leonard and Chani Grunstein,
in memory of Leonard's father,
Moshe Yonasan ben Yehuda Aryeh Leib, z"l,
father-in-law, Aharon ben Yitzchak, z"l
(Aron Tambor)
and brother,
Zvi Mayer ben Moshe Yonasan, z"l
(Harry Grunstein).*

David and Ruth Musher, in honor of their grandchildren

Ruth and Philip Roth, in memory of their son, Jonathan

*With profound gratitude to the Chaverim
of the Beit Midrash of Teaneck, whose shared
learning is an inspiration to our entire community.*

Beth and Morris Apfelbaum
Rabbi Meier Brueckheimer
Esther and Myron Chaitovsky
Esther and Nechemia Crystal
Dr. Larry and Toby Feder
Judy and Robert Friedman
Howard and Rochelle Gans
Len and Estee Goldsmith
Leonard and Chani Grunstein
Ruby and Bobby Kaplan
Joseph and Susan Penkower Kaplan
Dr. Chaim and Faye Feldman Kranzler
Tim and Ria Levart
Carl and Sara Markowitz
Carol and Danny Metzger
Jay and Penina Orlinsky
Zvi and Ida Plotzker
Aaron and Jean Rothstein
Esther and Jacob Schlanger
Sy Schulman
Yisrael Silverman
Dr. Norman Sohn
Yehuda and Fay Weiss

Jewish Center of Teaneck Rabbi's Fund

Contents

Foreword	xi
Introduction to the Psalms	1
Psalm 1: Reward and Punishment in the Book of Psalms	15
Psalms 3, 6, 30, 51: Transitions and Expansions Within Psalms	27
Psalms 9–10: Two Psalms or One?	37
Psalms 14–53: Redundant Psalms?	45
Psalm 19: Nature and Torah	51
Psalms 18, 57, 59, 63, 142: David and Saul in the Psalms	59
Psalm 51: David's Repentance from His Sin with Bathsheba and Uriah	73
God Insists on Truth: Rabbinic Evaluations of Two Audacious Biblical Prayers	83
Psalms 90–107: Rebuilding Faith After Crisis	93
Psalm 104: Interpretation of the Creation Narratives in Genesis	103
Psalms 113–118: *Hallel*	117
Psalms 121, 126: Journeys and Redemption	127
Psalm 145: Pure Praise	133

Foreword

About fifteen years ago, I was chatting with my then seven-year-old nephew. At that time, my nephew was a second grader in a local Yeshiva Day School. Although we had been discussing baseball, he suddenly interjected that "it matters what the words of the Torah mean, but it does not matter what the words of the prayers mean."

I was thunderstruck by this innocent yet profound observation. My nephew was reflecting what his religious education silently conveyed: His school devoted significant class time to learning the meaning of the Torah's words, yet prayer remained little more than a rote recital. (Update: my nephew, who now is 22, has developed a singular prayerful soul and elevates his community regularly by leading prayer services.)

That conversation triggered a deep memory. My journey with the Book of Psalms began when I was an eighteen-year-old yeshiva student in Israel after High School. Early in my first year, I noticed that many of the rabbis as well as students seemed genuinely connected to their prayers and were in no hurry to race through the prayers and move on with their day. Whatever they were experiencing was completely foreign to me. I suddenly felt a profound void in my understanding of prayer after a lifetime of Jewish education. So I took a Book of Psalms off the shelf and began reading it with an English translation and rabbinic commentary. Given that the prayer book is replete with psalms, this seemed like the best place to begin.

That turned out to be a life-transforming experience. I was mesmerized by the God-intoxication, the authenticity, the staggering courage and honesty, and the fiery religious passion in the psalms. Although prayer in school had been a mechanical exercise, I now was experiencing a world of genuine prayer.

When I began teaching advanced undergraduate Bible courses at Yeshiva University in 1996, I chose to teach Psalms as my second course. Engagement with the biblical text, classical commentaries, and contemporary scholarship was a markedly different experience from my initial encounter with Psalms at age 18. In this new setting as a teacher, learning preceded prayer.

Learning Psalms is quite unlike learning every other biblical book. Our goal remains one of Torah learning, but in Psalms that agenda must be a means to an ends, resulting in more authentic prayer. It is my hope and prayer that this companion volume will serve as a tool to enable readers of all backgrounds to understand the psalms, and through that learning to connect more to God through the experience of prayer.

* * *

Classical rabbinic commentary always forms the foundation of my learning. These towering individuals combine first-rate scholarship with intense religious commitment. The main commentators I have used on Psalms are Rabbi Shelomo Yitzhaki (Rashi, 1040–1105, Northern France), Rabbi Abraham ibn Ezra (1089–1164, Spain, Italy), Rabbi David Kimhi (Radak, 1160–c. 1235, Provence), Rabbi Isaiah of Trani (c. 1180–1250, Italy), Rabbi Menahem HaMeiri (1249–1316, Provence), Rabbi Joseph Hayyun (15th century, Portugal), Rabbis David and Hillel Altschuler (Metzudat David, 18th century Prague, Galicia), Rabbi Samson Raphael Hirsch (1808–1888, Germany), and Rabbi Meir Leibush ben Yehiel Michel (Malbim, 1809–1879, Romania, Germany).

Among modern commentaries, Amos Hakham's magisterial *Da'at Mikra* commentary (Mossad HaRav Kook, 1979) is an invaluable resource, as is Rabbi Elhanan Samet's *Iyyunim BeMizmorei Tehillim* (Yediot Aharonot, 2012).

I also benefited from Professor Uriel Simon's book, *Four Approaches to the Book of Psalms: From Saadiah Gaon to Abraham ibn Ezra* (New York: SUNY Press, 1991). Simon discusses the perspectives of Rabbi Saadiah Gaon (882–942, Babylonia), Rabbi Moshe ibn Gikatilla (11th century, Spain), Rabbi Abraham ibn Ezra, and also the medieval Karaite approach represented by Salmon ben Yeruham and Yefet ben Ali.

In addition to the classical rabbinic commentaries, I draw substantially from contemporary scholarship. I cite these scholars throughout this volume.

* * *

As always, thank you to my family for your love and encouragement: Mom and Dad; Ronda, Dan, Andrew, Jonathan, and Jeremy; Elana, Jamie, Jake, Max, Charlie, and Kara; Momma, Papap, Matt, Erin, Molly, and Emily; Nate, Kasey, Grace, and Jacob.

A particular word of gratitude to my father, Rabbi Marc D. Angel, and the Institute for Jewish Ideas and Ideals (jewishideas.org) for giving me the opportunity to channel scholarship and teaching that promote the core value issues that should shape our communal discourse and religious development. In my role as the National Scholar of the Institute, I teach in communities nationwide, run teacher trainings, and speak at universities. The Institute fosters an inclusive, scholarly, and spiritual Judaism that is faithful to tradition and that allows diverse Jews many different avenues of access into religious experience. I thank our Board and supporters for helping to turn our vision into a reality through our extensive programming and writings.

Thank you to my dear friends, who have helped sponsor this book: The Bengualid Family Foundation, Leonard and Chani Grunstein, David and Ruth Musher, and Ruth and Philip Roth. Your generosity enables our Institute to disseminate our vision to an ever-growing audience.

Thank you to the participants in the Beit Midrash of Teaneck, with whom I have learned twice weekly for over three years and who have built an exhilarating learning environment. It has been a singular privilege learning with you.

Thank you to Rabbi Alec Goldstein and Kodesh Press. Rabbi Goldstein has published several of my books and continues his tradition of careful editing and preparation of each volume.

Most importantly, I thank my wife Maxine, and our children Aviva, Dahlia, Mordechai, and Eliyahu for their infinite love and support. For the past three years, Maxine and I have chosen to homeschool our children. I am blessed with the privilege of learning religious studies with our children. The first thing we learn are the central prayers and their meaning, and we regularly pray together as a family. It is thrilling that our eleven-year-old daughters, Aviva and Dahlia, have chosen on their own initiative to create an activity book about the prayers as part of their Bat Mitzvah project. Last year we held a Siddur party for our seven-year-old son Mordechai, and currently are planning a Siddur party for our five-year-old son Eliyahu. I pray that our children continue to grow and develop, each in his and her individual way, into educated, thoughtful, God-fearing Jews whose prayers, learning, and actions contribute meaningfully to our community and beyond.

Turning to Maxine, I thank God many times each day that we have been blessed to be married for over twelve years. I would say that Maxine was the answer to all my prayers, but the truth is that I never even imagined or prayed for something this spectacular. Thank you for our singular marriage, for partnering with me in every way in raising our children, and for building an ever-stronger and more loving relationship together.

Hayyim Angel
March 17, 2022
Purim, 5782
Teaneck, New Jersey

Introduction to the Psalms

Although we refer to the *book* of Psalms as though it is one book, it is in fact divided into five collections: Psalms 1–41, 42–72, 73–89, 90–106, and 107–150. Perhaps the editors purposefully organized it into five collections to create a parallel with the Torah:

> All that Moses did, David also did… Moses gave five books of the Torah to Israel, and David gave the five books of Psalms to Israel (*Midrash Psalms* 1:2).[1]

Aside from noting the structural similarity, this Midrash parallels the two most important figures in Tanakh. Moses is the master of prophecy, and David is the master of prayer. Tanakh contains prophecy, which is the word of God to people; and wisdom, which is the word of people to other people. Psalms is the only book in Tanakh primarily representing the voice of people to God.

From the very beginnings of human history, people reach out to God through sacrifice (Cain and Abel) and prayer (from the time of Enosh, Genesis 4:25–26). While there are many rules and regulations for sacrifices and the Temple ritual in the Torah, there are none about prayer. The Torah does not explicitly command prayer at all,[2] but

---

Parts of this essay are adapted from Hayyim Angel, "Authorship and Structure of Psalms," in Angel, *Vision from the Prophet and Counsel from the Elders: A Survey of Nevi'im and Ketuvim* (New York: OU Press, 2013), pp. 210–219.

rather presents it as a spontaneous religious act during times of distress, petition, and gratitude.

With the elimination of sacrifices after the destruction of the Second Temple, prayer has taken on that ritualized role, as well. One talmudic passage captures the dual role of prayer, emulating the Patriarchs, but also corresponding to the sacrificial order:

> It has been stated: R. Jose son of R. Hanina said: The prayers were instituted by the Patriarchs. R. Joshua b. Levi says: The prayers were instituted to replace the daily sacrifices (*Berakhot* 26b).

We cannot know if the psalms were composed initially from a spontaneous reaction to particular events, or whether they were inspired prayers composed to be recited as ritual liturgy. Regardless, they may be interpreted in multiple ways to address people in different circumstances, as we shall see in our analysis of individual psalms.

AUTHORSHIP OF THE PSALMS

Of the 150 psalms in the Masoretic Text, seventy-three contain David's name in their superscriptions (introductory verses). Asaph appears in twelve, the Sons of Korah in eleven, Solomon in two (72, 127), Moses in one (90), and Ethan the Ezrahite in one (89). Three psalms mention Jeduthun in their superscriptions (39, 62, 77). Of those, Psalms 39 and 62 also mention David, and Psalm 77 also mentions Asaph. Heman the Ezrahite is mentioned in 88 along with the sons of Korah. Forty-nine psalms have no name in their superscriptions and of those forty-nine, twenty-four have no introductory formula at all.

Several commentators explore the identities of the figures mentioned in the superscriptions. Asaph was a leading Levite musician in David's time (see 1 Chronicles 16:7–33). Following midrashic traditions,[3] Rashi (on Psalm 42:1) asserts that the "Sons of Korah" refer to Korah's actual three sons (see Exodus 6:24). In contrast, Ibn Ezra (on Psalm 42:1) and many others maintain that the "Sons of Korah" are descendants of Korah.

The two Solomon psalms could have been composed by the wise king. However, some commentators maintain that the concluding verse of Psalm 72, "End of the prayers of David son of Jesse" (72:20), indicates that David composed this psalm on behalf of Solomon (Rashi, Ibn Ezra, Meiri on 72:1). Alternatively, Solomon could have composed the psalm (Targum, *Song of Songs Rabbah* 4:4), and 72:20 is a concluding verse for Book 2 added by the editors of the book of Psalms.

At the time of David, there were Levite singers named Heman, Ethan (1 Chronicles 6:16–32), and Jeduthun (1 Chronicles 16:41–42; 25:1–6). It is possible that the names that appear in those psalms refer to those individuals (Ibn Ezra). Alternatively, Rashi suggests that the "Ezrahite" appellation for Heman and Ethan in Psalms 88–89 means "from Zerah of the Tribe of Judah," based on the identification in 1 Chronicles 2:6, and these were different people from the Levites mentioned in 1 Chronicles 6. Although there was a Levite singer named Jeduthun, the expression *le-Yedutun* (of Jeduthun) appears in 39:1, whereas *al Yedutun* (on Jeduthun) is used in 62:1 and 77:1. That latter expression suggests an instrument or rhythm rather than a person. Given that all three Jeduthun psalms have the name of another individual (David or Asaph), it is difficult to clarify this reference.

Only two superscriptions explicitly date their psalms to a time other than that of David. Psalm 90 is ascribed to Moses, and Psalm 137 was composed "by the rivers of Babylon," referring to the Babylonian exile after the destruction of the First Temple in 586 BCE, some 400 years after David.

SUMMARY CHART OF THE PSALMS

Here is a chart that shows the distribution of names and other information in the superscriptions:

Books 1–3	Book 4	Book 5
David (3–41, 51–70, 86) 39 and 62 have Jeduthun also	Moses (90)	David (108–110, 138–145)
Asaph (50, 73–83) 77 has Jeduthun also	David (101, 103)	Two Hallelujah collections (111–113; 146–150) Three psalms without superscriptions (114–116)
Sons of Korah (42, 44–49, 84–85, 87–88) 88 has Heman the Ezrahite also		Hallelujah (117, 135) followed by "Praise the Lord for He is good" (118, 136)
Solomon (72) Ethan the Ezrahite (89)	For the Sabbath day (92) Of Thanksgiving (100) Of the lowly man (102)	"HaGomel" (107) Praise of the Torah (119) Song of Ascents (120–134, including four David, one Solomon) By the Rivers of Babylon (137)
Untitled (1, 2, 10, 33, 43, 66, 67, 71)	Untitled (91, 93–99, 104–106)	

THE RABBINIC SAGES

The Sages offer several approaches to the authorship and editing of the book of Psalms.

> David wrote the book of Psalms, including in it the work of the elders, namely, Adam, Melchizedek, Abraham, Moses, Heman, Jeduthun, Asaph, and the three sons of Korah.... Why is not Ethan the Ezrahite also reckoned with? Ethan the Ezrahite is Abraham... (*Bava Batra* 14b–15a).

In this passage, "wrote" can mean "authored," or "edited," or "committed oral traditions to writing." All of the people on this list either preceded or were contemporaneous with David. This passage midrashically identifies the Ethan the Ezrahite of Psalm 89 with Abraham. It also identifies the "Sons of Korah" with Korah's actual three sons. This rabbinic teaching considers David as the author of many of the psalms as well as the final editor of the book.

A different rabbinic tradition allows for post-David dating of psalms:

> Ten men composed the book of Psalms: Adam, Abraham, Moses, David, and Solomon – these are five.... Who are the other five?... Rav said: Asaph, Heman and Jeduthun, and the three sons of Korah and Ezra. Rabbi Johanan said: Asaph, Heman and Jeduthun are only one; add to them the three sons of Korah and Ezra (*Song of Songs Rabbah* 4:4).

Rav and Rabbi Johanan include Ezra in their list of authors, meaning that psalms were composed throughout the biblical period, even after David. The final formation of the book would have been done either by Ezra or the Men of the Great Assembly. This Midrash also claims that nobody disputes Solomon's inclusion on the list, but he is not included on the list in *Bava Batra*. Melchizedek is also not on this list, though he appears in *Bava Batra*. Finally, David is counted among the ten, instead of being listed in addition to ten others in *Bava Batra*.

In one of his introductions to Psalms, Ibn Ezra quotes the Sages as attributing the composition to the Men of the Great Assembly:

> Who composed this book? There is no need to answer, seeing that our Sages have said that the Men of the Great Assembly composed it. That is sufficient for us.

No extant rabbinic source states what Ibn Ezra claims,[4] though his position dovetails with *Song of Songs Rabbah* in emphasizing the later endpoint of authorship. Rabbi Eliyahu of Vilna (Gra on Proverbs 24:23) suggests that while the Men of the Great Assembly did not originally author the psalms, they were the final editors, organized the collections, and added the superscriptions.

A third view found among the Sages is that of Rabbi Meir:

> Rabbi Meir used to say: All the praises which are stated in the Book of Psalms, David uttered all of them, for it is said, "End of [*kollu*] the prayers of David son of Jesse" (Psalm 72:20): read not *kollu* [end of] but *kol ellu* [all these] (*Pesahim* 117a).

Differing from the first two sources that posit a multiplicity of authors, Rabbi Meir ascribes all psalms to David. He bases his assumption on a midrashic reading of Psalm 72:20 that is the opposite of the plain meaning of the verse. Nevertheless, the notion that David composed all the psalms became widespread over time.

POST-TALMUDIC COMMENTARY

Although Rabbi Meir did not elaborate on his attribution of all psalms to David, especially despite superscriptions that suggest otherwise, Rabbi Saadiah Gaon (882–942) did offer a theory of Davidic authorship in his commentary on Psalms. He asserted that all psalms are prophecies rather than prayers, and that David composed all of them. The other names that appear in the superscriptions refer to singers, musicians, or descendants of the named people. For example, Rabbi Saadiah maintains that David composed Psalm 90. "To Moses" refers to the Levitic descendants of Moses at the time of David, to whom David assigned this psalm to perform in the Temple.

It is possible that Rabbi Saadiah adopted this radical interpretation in the context of anti-Karaite polemics. Uriel Simon observes that the Karaites opposed rabbinic prayers and condemned the Sages for composing prayers that became the heart of Jewish liturgy. By placing the Amidah at the center of Jewish prayer, the Sages marginalized the divinely inspired psalms and replaced them with prayers of human origin. To counter this accusation, Rabbi Saadiah responded that it was necessary for the Sages to compose these prayers because the psalms are prophecies and therefore unsuitable to fill the role of prayer.[5] Regardless, the preponderance of commentators rejected Rabbi Saadiah's approach. They all understand psalms to be prayers.

Rabbi Moshe ibn Gikatilla (eleventh century) adopted an approach starkly different from that of Rabbi Saadiah. He maintained that none of the psalms prophetically predict or anticipate events. Therefore, one must examine their content to determine which events inspired them.

Ibn Gikatilla argues that the expression *le-David* (of David) in superscriptions can either mean that David authored the psalm, or that someone else wrote the psalm in David's honor ("ode to David"). Those psalms that do not contain David's name could have been written after David's time. He presumes that anonymous psalms were not written by David. The psalms ascribed to Asaph and the Sons of Korah may also refer to their descendants and not always the Levites who were David's contemporaries. For example, Psalm 79, ascribed to Asaf, appears to reflect the period of the destruction of the Temple. Therefore, it may have been composed by descendants of Asaf. These figures may have authored these psalms, as opposed to Rabbi Saadiah's opinion that David composed all of them.[6]

Ibn Ezra (1089–1164) adopted a more cautious position than Ibn Gikatilla. Some psalms might prophetically anticipate events but it is not necessary that any of them do. Ibn Ezra also suggests that while anonymous psalms need not have been composed by David, they might have been. Conversely, some of the psalms with David's name in the superscription may not have been written by David, but rather, in his honor (e.g., Psalm 20).

Ibn Ezra's concept of prophetic anticipation is not the same as Rabbi Saadiah's view. According to Ibn Ezra, psalms are not prophecies written in the form of a prayer. Rather, they are prayers composed in anticipation of later events for later generations to use.

We may use the superscription of Psalm 137, "By the rivers of Babylon," as a litmus test to illustrate how each of these commentators would respond to a psalm that evidently derives from a period centuries after David's time. Rabbi Saadiah argues that this psalm was composed by David through prophecy. It is as though David wrote: Thus says the Lord, there will be a destruction of the Temple and exile one day, and you will be miserable and desire revenge against your enemies. The psalm sounds like a lamentation, but is really a prophecy in the form of a lament.

Ibn Gikatilla submits that this psalm was composed by Jews in the Babylonian exile, lamenting their plight. Ibn Ezra suggests that this view of Ibn Gikatilla is plausible, but it is also possible that David prophetically foresaw the Babylonian exile and therefore composed this psalm to be used by those exiles as a prayer when the exile came. Ibn Ezra's first view is the same as Ibn Gikatilla's; his second view is not shared by Rabbi Saadiah. Rather, Ibn Ezra suggests that the psalm is a prayer written through prophetic anticipation.

Despite the diversity of traditional views on the authorship of Psalms, over time many came to believe that the "traditional" view of authorship was that David wrote all the psalms. In the nineteenth century, when German academic Bible Criticism challenged many traditional assumptions about the authorship of biblical books, many scholars rejected Davidic authorship of the book of Psalms by pointing to the superscription of Psalm 137, "By the rivers of Babylon," since the Babylonian exile happened after David. Many believers insisted that David must have prophesied that psalm, but many others sensed a conflict and erroneously concluded that there was a discrepancy between faith in the traditional view and the text evidence.

In his introduction to the book of Psalms, Malbim (1809–1879) censures people of faith and the critics alike. Jewish tradition does not demand belief in Davidic authorship or editing of the entire book of Psalms. Malbim adds that the assertion that David prophetically received Psalm 137 and included it in the book of Psalms also creates a problem of free will, since the existence of the psalm in Tanakh would make the destruction of the Temple set in stone some 400 years prior to the actual event. What would have happened had the people repented and avoided the destruction? Would the people then delete this psalm from Tanakh? In addition to Malbim's concern, there is an issue of relevance. How would people in David's time understand or use a psalm describing a future catastrophe?

After his discussion that essentially espouses the view of *Song of Songs Rabbah* and Ibn Ezra in understanding the book of Psalms as composed throughout the biblical period, Malbim relates his personal belief that David could have received these psalms with prophetic foresight and then kept them secret until the events occurred.[7] Amos Hakham takes the first point of Malbim's analysis for granted. People composed and edited psalms through the period of the Men of the Great Assembly and those are divinely inspired prayers.[8] These views accurately reflect biblical and talmudic-midrashic traditions.

In the twenty-first century, the myth of Davidic authorship as the "traditional" view continues to be perpetuated on both sides. Many traditionalists continue to teach that David was the author of Psalms. Academic scholars continue to assert wrongly that the traditional view was that David composed all of the psalms. Louis Jacobs used Psalm 137 as a precedent to challenge traditional views of authorship of other biblical books.[9] Christine Hayes remarked: "Tradition attributes the entire book of Psalms to King David.... However... some [Psalms] are clearly postexilic, such as... Psalm 137.... Despite the claim of religious tradition, the psalms were not all penned by David."[10] Similarly, James Kugel states that "Tradition assigns authorship to King David." He likewise appeals to the contents of Psalm 137 to explain how nineteenth-century scholars began to doubt this traditional assumption and ultimately rejected it.[11] This misconception creates a putative faith-text evidence conflict, when in fact none exists.

SUMMARY PRINCIPLES

According to traditional commentators, a superscription that says *le-David* (of David), or *le-Asaph* (of Asaph), etc., potentially has a range of meanings: (1) The psalm was written by this person or people. (2) The psalm was written in his or their honor by contemporaries or by later individuals. (3) The psalm was written by someone for the named people to sing or conduct. (4) The psalm was written by their descendants, or for their descendants to sing or to conduct.[12] (5) The psalm was written by that person, but could have been updated by a later writer.[13]

Having considered the biblical evidence, midrashic opinions, and later rabbinic commentary, we may derive several overarching principles of traditional interpretation: (1) The psalms were written and included in Tanakh with divine inspiration. (2) The book of Psalms expanded in content and form until the end of the period of Tanakh, until Ezra and the Men of the Great Assembly. (3) Whether a name appears on a psalm or not, we do not generally know who originally wrote the psalm, or if it was updated by later writers. (4) We generally do not know what event, if any, might have inspired the composition of a given psalm; psalms may have been composed initially as prayers for many occasions. (5) In theory, any psalm might prophetically anticipate an event, but none of them need to, and there never is reason to assume that any in fact do. (6) What matters most is what the psalm means and how it can be used as a prayer. These principles are helpful in understanding individual psalms and the book as a whole.

SING HIM A NEW SONG

Let us return to our earlier discussion about the Karaite protest against the Sages' composing new prayers and supplanting the inspired prayers in Psalms. Rabbi Saadiah's polemical stance against the Karaites regarding the nature of the book of Psalms – that it is comprised of prophecies not prayers – was admirable. However, Rabbi Saadiah's answer is unsatisfying, since our tradition uses the psalms as prayers, and this understanding appears patently correct in the text.

Offering a different response to the Karaite challenge, Amos Hakham responds that the book of Psalms contains beautiful poetry, but it often is difficult to understand. Additionally, many themes might be contained in a single psalm. Therefore, the Sages composed their prayers in simple Hebrew that could be understood by everyone, modeling their prayers after the Psalms and other verses in Tanakh.[14]

On a more conceptual level, the book of Psalms calls for people to compose new songs for God:

> Sing Him a new song; play sweetly with shouts of joy (Psalm 33:3; cf. 40:4; 96:1; 98:1; 144:9; 149:1).

Through their composition of liturgy, the Sages epitomize the relationship between the Written Law and the Oral Law. They capture the spirit of prayer from these psalms by composing their own, new prayers. By placing rabbinic prayers at the center of our liturgy, they demonstrate the need for human input and personalization of prayers. In contrast, the Karaites had no difficulty with the creation of the book of Psalms itself. Once that book was closed, however, they insisted that there was no room for new prayers.

Both sides of the debate are consistent with their general worldviews. The Karaites froze the biblical text, whereas the Sages captured its inner essence and used Psalms to teach us how to pray. Amos Hakham observes that the book of Psalms encourages people to continue this vibrant process of prayer:

> "Sing Him a new song" (Psalm 33:3):… it is likely that the verse means that it is worthy to sing a truly new song to God. The large number of Psalms attests to the fact that our predecessors composed new songs from time to time.[15]

> "Sing to the Lord a new song…" (Psalm 149:1) intimates that even though we are approaching the conclusion of the book, we have not concluded all praises of God, and we are yet obligated to sing new songs to God. Indeed, each generation produced God-fearing individuals who composed new prayers, poems, and praises to God.[16]

Thus, the Karaites reflect their Written Law emphasis, whereas the Sages and later rabbinic tradition model the dynamic relationship between the Written and Oral Law, and how that impacts on prayer.

NOTES

1. Amos Hakham (*Da'at Mikra: Psalms* vol. 1 [Hebrew] [Jerusalem: Mossad HaRav Kook, 1979], introduction, p. 3) observes that in some old manuscripts of Psalms, several lines separate each book, like in the Torah.
2. Rambam (*Hilkhot Tefillah* 1:1) derives a positive commandment to pray from verses in the Torah, whereas other authorities maintain that prayer is generally a rabbinic commandment. The Sages also derive a positive commandment for the Grace after Meals from Deuteronomy 8:10, "When you have eaten your fill, give thanks to the Lord your God for the good land which He has given you."
3. For example, *Bava Batra* 14b–15a, *Song of Songs Rabbah* 4:4.
4. Uriel Simon (*Four Approaches to the Book of Psalms: From Saadiah Gaon to Abraham ibn Ezra* [New York: SUNY Press, 1991], p. 184) assumes that Ibn Ezra erred in his quotation of the talmudic passage in *Bava Batra* because Ibn Ezra frequently wandered and did not have access to his library. At any rate, Ibn Ezra's view fundamentally approaches that of *Song of Songs Rabbah*.
5. Simon, *Four Approaches to the Book of Psalms*, introduction p. ix; pp. 8, 11.
6. Rabbi Tanhum HaYerushalmi (13th century, Egypt) adopts a similar approach. He maintains that Psalm 137, and several lamentations, especially in book 3, were composed during the Babylonian exile. Like Rabbi Moshe ibn Gikatilla, he assumed that Asaph or the Sons of Korah can refer to their descendants (Aryeh Tzoref, "Tanhum HaYerushalmi and Rabbi Moshe ben Gikatilla on the Superscriptions of the Psalms and Their Authors" [Hebrew], *Sinai* 149 [2016], pp. 73–91).
7. Yoshi Farajun notes that in the first edition of Malbim's commentary on Psalms, this footnote did not appear. Farajun surmises that Malbim added it later in response to criticism of his idea from more conservative rabbis (in Yehudah Brandes, Tovah Ganzel, Hayutah Deutsch editors, *BeEnei Elohim VaAdam: HaAdam HaMa'amin UMehkar HaMikra* [Hebrew] [Jerusalem: Beit Morasha, 2015], p. 78, n. 143).
8. Amos Hakham, *Da'at Mikra: Psalms* vol. 1, pp. 9–13.
9. Louis Jacobs, *Beyond Reasonable Doubt* (Oxford, Portland OR: The Littman Library of Jewish Civilization, 2004), pp. 15–16, 32–35, 39, 47–51, 61.
10. Christine Hayes, *Introduction to the Bible* (New Haven, CT: Yale University Press, 2012), p. 346.
11. James L. Kugel, *How to Read the Bible: A Guide to Scripture, Then and Now* (New York: Free Press, 2007), pp. 459–461.
12. For example, Radak and Malbim maintain that Psalms 82–83 were written by a descendant of Asaph based on the content of those psalms which suggests a later date. Rabbi Moshe ibn Gikatilla also considers many of the

psalms ascribed to Asaph or the Sons of Korah to have been composed by their descendants. For example, Psalm 79 is "of Asaph" but appears to reflect the period of the destruction of the Temple.

13. For example, Tosafot (*Yevamot* 64b) are bothered by Psalm 90:10, "The span of our life is seventy years, or, given the strength, eighty years." If Moses authored this psalm and lived to 120, why would he offer an average life expectancy of seventy or eighty? The Tosafists therefore consider this verse a later addition by David, who lived to be seventy. Ibn Ezra, Radak, and Meiri are not bothered by this question, since Moses could say that most people still live to seventy or eighty, rather than 120. Malbim also maintains that Psalm 53 is modeled after Psalm 14 but was updated slightly by Hezekiah.
14. Hakham, *Da'at Mikra: Psalms* vol. 1, introduction, p. 49.
15. Hakham, *Da'at Mikra: Psalms* vol. 1, p. 181, n. 4.
16. Hakham, *Da'at Mikra: Psalms* vol. 2, p. 606.

Psalm 1:
Reward and Punishment in the Book of Psalms

The final editors of Psalms had to choose one of the 150 to introduce the book. Aside from Psalm 1, several other psalms are addressed to other people rather than to God (e.g., 4, 37, 49, 62). Nevertheless, it is interesting that the first psalm is not a prayer to God, but rather is wisdom from the psalmist to his audience. Most psalms express words of prayer to God.

> Happy is the man who has not followed the counsel of the wicked, or taken the path of sinners, or joined the company of the insolent; rather, the teaching of the Lord is his delight, and he studies that teaching day and night. He is like a tree planted beside streams of water, which yields its fruit in season, whose foliage never fades, and whatever it produces thrives. Not so the wicked; rather, they are like chaff that wind blows away. Therefore the wicked will not survive judgment, nor will sinners, in the assembly of the righteous. For the Lord

---

This chapter is adapted from Hayyim Angel, "The Differences between the Wise the Foolish in Psalms: Theodicy, Understanding Providence, and Religious Responses," in Angel, *Creating Space between Peshat and Derash: A Collection of Studies on Tanakh* (Jersey City, NJ: Ktav-Sephardic Publication Foundation, 2011), pp. 163–172.

cherishes the way of the righteous, but the way of the wicked is doomed (Psalm 1).

Radak (on Psalm 1:1) suggests that the book of Psalms begins with this proclamation of faith because of the importance of the themes of reward-punishment and divine providence:

> In this psalm, David included the laws of man and what should happen to him in this world, that is, the reward for the righteous and punishment for the wicked. This psalm is very exalted, and therefore he began his book with it.

Belief in providence and justice is critical for prayer in general.[1]

Amos Hakham suggests another reason for the primary position of Psalm 1. It is an exhortation – those approaching God must be righteous.[2] Nahum Sarna adds that Psalm 1 stresses Torah study (v. 2), treating it as an act of profound worship in addition to prayer.[3] Thus Psalm 1 makes for an excellent opening to the book of Psalms, because it creates the religious foundation upon which many psalms are based.[4]

DIVINE JUSTICE IN PSALMS

Several psalms are based on the assumption that the person praying is righteous and therefore worthy of salvation. To cite two examples:

> The Lord rewarded me according to my merit; He requited the cleanness of my hands; for I have kept to the ways of the Lord, and have not been guilty before my God; for I am mindful of all His rules; I have not disregarded His laws (Psalm 18:21–22).

> Preserve my life, for I am steadfast; O You, my God, deliver Your servant who trusts in You. Have mercy on me, O Lord, for I call to You all day long (Psalm 86:2–3).

Another psalmist appeals to the fact that he prays to God as the reason why God should save him:

Protect me and save me; let me not be disappointed, for I have sought refuge in You. May integrity and uprightness watch over me, for I look to You (Psalm 25:20–21).

Amos Hakham observes that the psalmists in the above passages are not bragging about their righteousness so much as teaching that even a divinely chosen king is obligated to remain faithful to God.[5] More significantly, these psalms highlight the principle of Psalm 1, that God upholds justice.[6]

However, there are other psalms that address the apparent discrepancies between the principle of divine fairness and the reality that the righteous sometimes suffer and the wicked sometimes prosper. Psalm 37 is concerned with people becoming demoralized by the success of the wicked and the suffering of the righteous: "Do not be vexed by evil men; do not be incensed by wrongdoers; for they soon wither like grass, like verdure fade away" (Psalm 37:1). Like Psalm 1, Psalm 37 argues that the success of the wicked is illusory. The tone of these two psalms, however, is notably different. Psalm 1 is a confident proclamation of faith, whereas Psalm 37 expresses concern with the success of the wicked and the need to defend belief in Divine reward and punishment. Additionally, Psalm 37 admits that there are temporary instances of unfairness. People must wait to witness ultimate justice.

Strikingly, Psalm 37 appeals to personal observation to verify its thesis: "I have been young and am now old, but I have never seen a righteous man abandoned, or his children seeking bread" (Psalm 37:25).[7] Several commentators cannot accept this statement at face value. Since there are times that righteous people face starvation, Ibn Ezra, Radak, and Meiri modify the verse to mean that the righteous are never *totally* abandoned. These commentators argue for some poetic flexibility as they attempt to bridge the literal reading of the verse with actual human experience.

Similarly, some commentators struggle with the sweeping formulations in Psalm 107:

Some lived in deepest darkness, bound in cruel irons, because they defied the word of God, spurned the counsel of the Most High. He humbled their hearts through suffering; they stumbled with no one to help (Psalm 107:10–12).

There were fools who suffered for their sinful way, and for their iniquities. All food was loathsome to them; they reached the gates of death (Psalm 107:17–18).

According to the literal reading of these verses, prison terms and illnesses should be attributed to sinful behavior. Rashi and Ibn Ezra therefore explain that anyone who is ill is called a fool (v. 17), since by definition he or she must have sinned. Ibn Ezra (on Psalm 107:11, 42) goes on to modify this principle based on human reality: *most* prisoners must have sinned, but it is possible that some have not and are being unjustly punished.

Radak explains 107:17 differently: "Had they been wise, they would think: why has God sent this illness upon us?...But fools are insensitive to this matter, and do not repent until their illness becomes very great." According to Radak, the primary difference between wise people and fools is that wise people who get ill utilize their illness as a religious opportunity for introspection and repentance, whereas fools do not. Thus, Radak frames the contrast between the wise and fools primarily as one of religious response, not as a guarantee of a higher quality of life or better health for the righteous.[8]

When God's principles of fairness are not evident in history, psalmists may petition God for salvation by invoking God's fairness, or they may even protest bitterly over the injustice. For example, Psalm 44 praises God for saving Israel in the past, but then protests Israel's current suffering and demands that God act for the sake of justice:

> Yet You have rejected and disgraced us; You do not go with our armies. You make us retreat before our foe; our enemies plunder us at will....All this has come upon us, yet we have not forgotten You, or been false to Your covenant....It is for Your sake that we are slain all day long, that we are regarded as

sheep to be slaughtered. Rouse Yourself; why do You sleep, O Lord? Awaken, do not reject us forever!…Arise and help us, redeem us, as befits Your faithfulness (Psalm 44:10–27).[9]

Perhaps the most unusual response to the suffering of the righteous is found in Psalm 94: "Happy is the man whom You discipline, O Lord, the man You instruct in Your teaching" (Psalm 94:12). Rather than calling upon his audience to wait patiently for ultimate justice, or insisting that the righteous never suffer, this psalmist views suffering as a sign of divine favor and loving attention.[10]

Moreover, Psalm 94 is unique in its rebuke of those who question God's supervision and fairness:

> Take heed, you most brutish people; fools, when will you get wisdom? Shall He who implants the ear not hear, He who forms the eye not see? Shall He who disciplines nations not punish, He who instructs men in knowledge? (Psalm 94:8–10).

In contrast, other psalmists do not criticize those who question God's justice, but rather attempt to resolve their doubts.

Psalm 1 sets out a simple principle of divine justice: righteous people flourish while evil people wither away. This approach presents a conflict with the reality that most people perceive. Below is a summary of the main approaches of the Psalms and the commentators toward addressing this apparent conflict:

1. Psalm 1 represents the reality. There are no conflicts, and wise people can perceive justice all the time (Psalm 37:25, 107:11).
2. In the end, all will be righted, so be patient (Psalm 1, 37). Psalm 37 explains this principle to a doubting audience.
3. The principles of justice should always be true, and therefore one should pray to God to apply them, or thank God after those principles are applied (Psalm 18:20–25; 86:2–3).
4. There are times when the world seems unfair, leading psalmists to either petition God or protest injustice (Psalm 44).
5. Suffering may be a sign of God's love rather than punishment (Psalm 94:12).

6. God's principles of justice apply *most* of the time (Ibn Ezra, Radak, Meiri on Psalm 37:25; Ibn Ezra on Psalm 107:11).
7. The wise use their suffering as a religious opportunity to reach out to God as well as to introspect, whereas fools abandon faith (Radak on Psalm 107:17).

THE CONCERNS OF PSALMISTS

Although the principles underlying Psalm 1 are affirmed by many psalmists, some present a religious struggle of the psalmist. For example, Psalm 39 opens with a raging internal battle as the psalmist attempts to restrain himself:

> I resolved I would watch my step lest I offend by my speech; I would keep my mouth muzzled while the wicked man was in my presence. I was dumb, silent; I was very still while my pain was intense. My mind was in a rage, my thoughts were all aflame; I spoke out (Psalm 39:2–4).

Amos Hakham explains that although the psalmist begins by trying to control himself, he eventually verbalizes his conflicts and does not reach any resolution. However, he remains steadfastly devoted to God through his suffering, praying that God eliminate his torments.[11]

Perhaps the most remarkable prayer addressing the conflict between the principle of fairness and human experience is Psalm 73, which presents the psalmist's personal struggle:

> As for me, my feet had almost strayed, my steps were nearly led off course, for I envied the wanton; I saw the wicked at ease.… It was for nothing that I kept my heart pure and washed my hands in innocence, seeing that I have been constantly afflicted, that each morning brings new punishments. Had I decided to say these things, I should have been false to the circle of Your disciples. So I applied myself to understand this, but it seemed a hopeless task till I entered God's sanctuary and reflected on their fate (Psalm 73:2–17).

This psalmist portrays himself as one who almost lost his faith as a result of witnessing the success of the wicked and enduring his own suffering.[12] Not until he entered God's sanctuary were his difficulties resolved (v. 17).[13] He proceeds to adopt the same response as that found in Psalms 1, 37, and others: the wicked ultimately will meet their doom (73:18–20).

Unlike other psalms that use patience as a resolution, however, Psalm 73 continues: "My mind was stripped of its reason, my feelings were numbed. I was a dolt, without knowledge; I was brutish toward You" (73:21–22). Although he had reached a resolution in verses 17–20, the psalmist breaks chronological boundaries with this flashback, indicating an ongoing religious struggle. It is also noteworthy that this conclusion was not as obvious to this psalmist as it is to the writers of Psalms 1 and 37. He needed to enter God's sanctuary after reaching a state of near-despair.

The conclusion of Psalm 73 suggests a different contrast between the wise and foolish from the approaches outlined above:

> Yet I was always with You, You held my right hand; You guided me by Your counsel and led me toward honor. Whom else have I in heaven? And having You, I want no one on earth. My body and mind fail; but God is the stay of my mind, my portion forever. Those who keep far from You perish; You annihilate all who are untrue to You. As for me, nearness to God is good; I have made the Lord God my refuge, that I may recount all Your works (Psalm 73:23–28).

The psalmist states that he is close to God (v. 23) whereas the wicked are distant from God (v. 27). The success of the wicked may be fleeting, but that is not the main resolution of Psalm 73. Instead, the psalmist uses his suffering and theological torment as an opportunity to draw closer to God.[14]

Rather than viewing this psalm as exceptional, one Midrash contends that Psalm 73 serves as a model for the rest of the Psalms, since it contains the true essence of the book of Psalms: "'I was a dolt, without knowledge, etc.' (73:22): This should have been the beginning of the book, but there is no chronological order in the Torah" (*Ecclesiastes Rabbah* 1:12). Instead of the confident declaration of faith in Psalm 1, the Sages of this Midrash appear to have considered the struggle of Psalm 73 to be central to the religious nature of the book of Psalms. The response of the wise and righteous individual contrasts with that of the wicked fool, even if both might live the same successful – or miserable – lifestyles. However, the wise do not necessarily perceive justice any more than fools do.

It might also be significant that Psalm 73 begins the third book of Psalms, and thus the second half of the book of Psalms. If so, the very structure of the book may waver between the confidence of Psalm 1, which begins the first half; and the uncertainty of Psalm 73, which begins the second half.[15] It must be stressed, however, that it is impossible to ascertain the underlying purposes of the current canonical arrangement of the Psalms, and therefore this suggestion of change in attitude belongs to the realm of intriguing speculation.

This tension between the potential primacy of Psalm 1 or Psalm 73 is captured poignantly by Radak's comments on Psalm 92. The verses read:

> How great are Your works, O Lord, how very subtle Your designs! A brutish man cannot know, a fool cannot understand this: though the wicked sprout like grass, though all evildoers blossom, it is only that they may be destroyed forever. But You are exalted, O Lord, for all time (Psalm 92:6–9).

Typically, these verses are understood as contrasting the wise and fools. Wise people are confident that the success of the wicked is illusory. In contrast, fools do not understand this truth (Rashi, Amos Hakham).[16] Radak, however, is unsure if 92:7 should be translated as "A brutish man cannot know" – whereas the wise man does know; or whether "man is a brute and cannot know," that is, *no* man – not even Moses our Teacher – can fathom the success of the wicked. This ambiguity resembles the tension between Psalm 1 and Psalm 73 as hypothetical competitors for the primary position in the book of Psalms. In the context of verses that appear to contrast the knowledge of the fools with that of the wise, Radak suggests that all people are fools when it comes to understanding God's ways.

CONCLUSION

There are two extremes depicted within the book of Psalms. Sometimes the wise person clearly understands God's ways whereas the fool does not. At other times, nobody – not even the psalmist – understands. Sometimes it is assumed that the righteous person necessarily will live a happier life than the wicked one, at least in the long run; at other times nobody can perceive Divine justice.

Yet there consistently remain two differences between the wise and the fool in Psalms. One is how they respond to conflicts between religious principles and perceived reality. Because of unfairness in this world, the wicked abandon God: "The benighted man thinks, 'God does not care'" (14:1). In contrast, the righteous develop their relationship with God, sometimes by remaining steadfast in their belief that everything must ultimately be fair, and sometimes by protesting or pleading. Whatever their response, they create a dynamic connection to God: "Yet I was always with You" (73:23), proclaims the troubled psalmist. The second is that wise people continually return to the beliefs set out in Psalm 1, whereas fools despair of God's ultimate justice.

Psalms offer various ways of approaching God in all situations, good and bad. These matters, of course, reach far beyond the simple meaning of verses in the book of Psalms – they shape the very nature of prayer and religious experience.

NOTES

1. Rabbi Yosef Hayyun (on Psalm 1:1) suggests further that Psalm 1 serves as an introduction to the entire book of Psalms.
2. Amos Hakham, *Da'at Mikra: Psalms* vol. 1 (Hebrew), (Jerusalem: Mossad HaRav Kook, 1979), pp. 5–6.
3. Nahum M. Sarna, *On the Book of Psalms: Exploring the Prayers of Ancient Israel* (New York: Schocken Books, 1993), pp. 26–29.
4. It is worth noting that the aforementioned commentators offer their explanations based on the current canonical form of the Psalms. However, the Talmud (*Berakhot* 9b–10a) suggests that Psalms 1–2 were initially combined. Notwithstanding, the book of Psalms' introduction with its opening verses still may be interpreted along the lines of Radak, Hakham, and Sarna.
5. Hakham, *Da'at Mikra: Psalms* vol. 1, pp. 85–87, 95–96.
6. Rabbinic tradition moved away from prayers that appeal to personal merit for salvation: "R. Johanan said in the name of R. Jose b. Zimra: If a man makes his petition depend on his own merit, heaven makes it depend on the merit of others; and if he makes it depend on the merit of others, heaven makes it depend on his own merit. Moses made his petition depend on the merit of others, as it says, 'Remember Abraham, Isaac and Israel Your servants!' (Exodus 32:13), and Scripture made it depend on his own merit, as it says, 'Therefore He said that He would destroy them, had not Moses His chosen stood before Him in the breach to turn back His wrath, lest He should destroy them' (Psalm 106:23). Hezekiah made his petition depend on his own merit, as it is written, 'Remember now, O Lord, I beseech You, how I have walked before You' (Isaiah 38:3), and God made it depend on the merit of others, as it says, 'For I will defend this city to save it, for My own sake and for My servant David's sake' (Isaiah 37:35)."
7. Psalm 92 similarly appeals to personal experience in verses 11–12 amidst a philosophical discussion. The psalmist achieves spiritual ecstasy through his reflection, and perhaps his personal salvation contributes to this religious state. For discussion of the development of this psalm and its ideas, see Nava Cohen, "Psalm 92: Structure and Meaning," *Zeitschrift für die Alttestamentliche Wissenschaft* 125 (2013), pp. 595–606.
8. Cf. Rabbi Joseph B. Soloveitchik, *Fate and Destiny: From the Holocaust to the State of Israel* (Hoboken, NJ: KTAV, 2000), 1–10.
9. For further expansion on this theme, see Karl N. Jacobson, "Perhaps Y-H-W-H is Sleeping: 'Awake' and 'Contend' in the Book of Psalms," in *The Shape and Shaping of the Book of Psalms: The Current State of Scholarship*, ed. Nancy L. deClaisse-Walford (Atlanta: SBL Press, 2014), pp. 129–145.
10. Cf. Deuteronomy 8:5: "Bear in mind that the Lord your God disciplines you just as a man disciplines his son." Cf. Proverbs 3:12; Job 5:17; 33:17–20.

See also *Berakhot* 5b, which maintains that it is a daily occurrence that some people suffer without sin.
11. Hakham, *Da'at Mikra: Psalms* vol. 1, p. 227.
12. Hakham (*Da'at Mikra: Psalms* vol. 2, p. 10) suggests that the psalmist may be speaking autobiographically, but it is also possible that he is speaking as a sage describing the experience of the many.
13. Hakham (*Da'at Mikra: Psalms* vol. 2, p. 6) interprets this verse to mean that by coming to the Temple precincts, the psalmist met with sages and prophets, who taught him the proper response.
14. See further discussion in J. Clinton McCann, Jr., "Psalm 73: A Microcosm of Old Testament Theology," in *The Listening Heart: Essays in Wisdom and the Psalms in honor of Roland E. Murphy*, ed. Kenneth G. Hoglund et al. (Sheffield: JSOT Press, 1987), pp. 247–257.
15. Cf. Walter Brueggemann and Patrick D. Miller, "Psalm 73 as a Canonical Marker," *Journal for the Study of the Old Testament* 72 (1996), pp. 45–56.
16. Hakham, *Da'at Mikra: Psalms* vol. 2, p. 181.

Psalms 3, 6, 30, 51: Transitions and Expansions Within Psalms

Many psalms transition from one theme or mood to another. In this chapter we consider different forms of transition and expansion as manifest in Psalms 3, 6, 30, and 51.

PSALM 3

A psalm of David when he fled from his son Absalom. O Lord, my foes are so many! Many are those who attack me; many say of me, "There is no deliverance for him through God." Selah.[1] But You, O Lord, are a shield about me, my glory, He who holds my head high. I cry aloud to the Lord, and He answers me from His holy mountain. Selah.

I lie down and sleep and wake again, for the Lord sustains me. I have no fear of the myriad forces arrayed against me on every side. Rise, O Lord! Deliver me, O my God! For You slap all my enemies in the face; You break the teeth of the wicked. Deliverance is the Lord's; Your blessing be upon Your people! Selah.

This chapter is adapted from my essay, "Transitions and Expansions in Psalms," in Angel, *Vision from the Prophet and Counsel from the Elders: A Survey of Nevi'im and Ketuvim* (New York: OU Press, 2013), pp. 220-226.

The first half of Psalm 3 is a cry for help, while the second half expresses confidence that God will save. Suddenly, the psalmist is able to sleep soundly as his worries vanish. What caused this abrupt shift? Ibn Ezra, Radak, and Meiri suggest that perhaps David received prophecy that he would be saved, or else time elapsed between the first half of the psalm when David still was in danger and the second half which he composed after he was saved. Their interpretations are rooted in the assumption that Psalm 3 is an actual transcript of a prayer David recited when fleeing Absalom.

However, it is possible that the change of tone within the psalm can be understood without assuming prophetic anticipation or a chronological gap. Throughout his commentary on Psalms, Amos Hakham (*Da'at Mikra*) regularly cites the Midrash: "Rabbi Yudan said in the name of Rabbi Yehudah: all that David said in his book was said for him and for all Israel and for all times" (*Midrash Psalms* 18:1). Even in psalms whose superscriptions specify events in David's life, the wording of the body of the psalm is always expressed in general terms. When fearful of Esau, Jacob prayed, "Deliver me, I pray, from the hand of my brother, from the hand of Esau" (Genesis 32:12). In contrast, even when the psalm's superscription specifically links the prayer to when David fled from his son Absalom, the psalm is formulated in general terms so that all people would be able to use it in their prayers.

Hakham argues that the fact that the psalmist is praying gives him greater faith and confidence, since he realizes that he is not alone.[2] From this vantage point, the psalm need not reflect a particular event in David's life.

In addition to the transition of the mental state of the psalmist, the final verse marks a shift from concern about a personal plight to a national setting. In this regard, Psalm 3 is not alone, as several psalms begin with an individual praying for personal needs and then subsequently expressing concern for the broader community (see, e.g., Psalms 51 and 130).

There is another possible transition in this psalm as well, depending on how one interprets its first word, *mizmor*. This term introduces fifty-seven psalms and appears nowhere in Tanakh outside of the book of Psalms. One Sage in the Talmud understands the term *mizmor* to mean "a happy song" (*Berakhot* 7b). From that perspective, it is difficult to say that David would begin a psalm that stems from feelings of despair with the word *mizmor*, which connotes joy. To rectify this difficulty, the Sage suggests that David knew from the prophet Nathan that there would be a rebellion from within David's home (II Samuel 12), and David was relieved to learn that the rebel was his son Absalom rather than someone else in his court. Rashi adopts this talmudic interpretation.

Ibn Ezra agrees with the Talmud that *mizmor* means "a happy song," but considers the rest of the talmudic interpretation beyond the textual evidence, and therefore should be considered *derash*. He suggests instead that the term *mizmor* is apt since the psalmist senses salvation midway through the prayer and becomes joyful. Radak also agrees that *mizmor* means "a happy song" but still views the psalm as a prayer stemming from distress. Consequently, he suggests that this psalm was not originally called *mizmor* when David first recited it. Only after David was saved, and the psalm was incorporated into the Temple liturgy, was it transformed into a psalm of gratitude. According to Radak, the psalm meant one thing when it was composed and another after it became part of the fixed prayer service.

In contrast, Meiri disagrees with the talmudic definition of *mizmor*, since some psalms such as 79 are distressing, and do not describe salvation at the end. Meiri insists that *mizmor* should be translated more neutrally as "a psalm," rather than "a happy song."

To summarize, this psalm may be used by someone in distress to petition God for salvation, and it also may be used by someone already saved from distress who thanks God for that salvation. The multiple meanings of the psalm make it eternally relevant.

PSALM 6

For the leader; with instrumental music on the *sheminith*. A psalm of David. O Lord, do not punish me in anger, do not chastise me in fury. Have mercy on me, O Lord, for I languish; heal me, O Lord, for my bones shake with terror. My whole being is stricken with terror, while You, Lord – O, how long! O Lord, turn! Rescue me! Deliver me as befits Your faithfulness. For there is no praise of You among the dead; in Sheol, who can acclaim You? I am weary with groaning; every night I drench my bed, I melt my couch in tears. My eyes are wasted by vexation, worn out because of all my foes.

Away from me, all you evildoers, for the Lord heeds the sound of my weeping. The Lord heeds my plea, the Lord accepts my prayer. All my enemies will be frustrated and stricken with terror; they will turn back in an instant, frustrated.

Psalm 6 describes an ill person who cries to God from distress. In this psalm, there is a thematic shift from illness to enemies. Ibn Ezra suggests that the psalm refers either to the psalmist's personal illness or to a prophecy of the exile. Radak suggests that Psalm 6 is written prospectively, and the psalmist could have prayed from personal illness, or perhaps he composed a prayer to be used by anyone who is sick. In contrast, Meiri views the psalm as retrospective, written from the vantage point of one who has already been healed and saved and now is looking back on his experiences with gratitude. The distress expressed at the beginning of the psalm flashes back to the prayer he recited while still ill. Like Psalm 3, Psalm 6 also can serve as a prayer from distress or a prayer of gratitude. Once again, the psalm illustrates how prayer transforms us. When we pray from distress, we no longer are alone and feel greater security by sensing God's Presence.

Rabbi Elhanan Samet[3] suggests an additional element of understanding the transition in Psalm 6. The first half of the psalm (verses 2–6) directly addresses God, whereas in the second half (verses 7–11), the psalmist speaks about God and his woes.

Generally in the book of Psalms, the turning point in a prayer resembles what we saw in psalm 3. The psalmist prays, that prayer brings God closer, and the psalmist feels like he has been heard and gains confidence for the second half of the psalm. In Psalm 6, however, the psalmist cries to himself at this point: "I am weary with groaning; every night I drench my bed, I melt my couch in tears. My eyes are wasted by vexation, worn out because of all my foes" (verses 7–8).

Rabbi Samet explains that people who pray from distress do not always feel like they have been heard, and the despair of the psalmist reflects that mood. He begins to cry, and no longer speaks directly to God.

The psalmist's tears melt the barrier he had felt with God, and finally by the end of the psalm he feels that God has heard him: "Away from me, all you evildoers, for the Lord heeds the sound of my weeping. The Lord heeds my plea, the Lord accepts my prayer. All my enemies will be frustrated and stricken with terror; they will turn back in an instant, frustrated" (verses 9–11).

PSALM 30

A psalm of David. A song for the dedication of the House. I extol You, O Lord, for You have lifted me up, and not let my enemies rejoice over me. O Lord, my God, I cried out to You, and You healed me. O Lord, You brought me up from Sheol, preserved me from going down into the Pit. O you faithful of the Lord, sing to Him, and praise His holy name. For He is angry but a moment, and when He is pleased there is life. One may lie down weeping at nightfall; but at dawn there are shouts of joy.

When I was untroubled, I thought, "I shall never be shaken," for You, O Lord, when You were pleased, made [me] firm as a mighty mountain. When You hid Your face, I was terrified. I called to You, O Lord; to my Lord I made appeal. "What is to be gained from my death, from my descent into the Pit? Can dust praise You? Can it declare Your faithfulness? Hear, O Lord, and have mercy on me; O LORD, be my help!" You turned my lament into dancing, you undid my sackcloth and girded me with joy, that [my] whole being might sing hymns to You endlessly; O Lord my God, I will praise You forever.

In Psalm 30, the psalmist opens with praises of God for saving him. As in Psalm 6, there are references both to illness and enemies. Amos Hakham offers several approaches to explaining the presence of both enemies and illness. (1) Everyone has enemies and they are maliciously happy when one becomes ill. (2) Illness may be used as a metaphor for enemies, or the other way around. (3) The psalm contains a roster of different maladies (enemies, illness, mourning) so that a variety of people may use this psalm when they are saved from different kinds of distress. There is no need to "harmonize" these references unless one assumes that a particular historical event inspired the composition of the psalm.[4]

Psalm 30 contains a different type of transition from those in Psalms 3 and 6. The psalmist already has been saved and thanks God. He then flashes back to reflect on his overconfident state prior to his maladies, "when I was untroubled…" (verse 7). He then speaks of how woes befell him and he then prayed for divine salvation, culminating in his rescue. The psalmist can thank God even more fully since he appreciates his journey now that it is behind him. The psalmist learns from the process and publicizes it so that others may learn from his experiences. He thanks God and also introspects.

The superscription of the psalm has presented a particular challenge for interpreters. It refers to the "dedication of the House," ostensibly a reference to the Temple. Of course, David was no longer alive when his son Solomon built and dedicated the Temple. Additionally, the contents of the psalm have little to do with a Temple dedication. It appears that the prayer revolves around salvation from mortal danger.

Rashi and Radak suggest that David must have received prophecy about the Temple and therefore was able to compose this psalm in advance. Ibn Ezra quotes Rabbi Moshe ibn Gikatilla, who suggests that David thanked God when Nathan told him that although he would not build the Temple, his son would (II Samuel 7). The danger in the psalm refers to David's initial depression over being prohibited to build the Temple, now overcome by joy over the news that his son would. Nevertheless, the psalm describes mortal danger, not sadness.

Ibn Ezra and Meiri submit that the psalm refers to the dedication of David's palace. David dedicated his palace after overcoming mortal danger. Malbim proposes that the "House" refers to David's body, which houses the soul (see, e.g., Ecclesiastes 12:3). In this metaphorical reading, David had been physically ill and then recovered. Rabbi Isaiah of Trani suggests that David knew that his son would build the Temple, and thanked God for saving him from his wars that would pave the way for the future Temple building. Rabbi Yosef Hayyun submits that *bayit* also can mean "dynasty." In Rabbi Hayyun's reading, David composed this psalm when the entire nation of Israel accepted him as king to begin his dynasty, and thanked God for saving him from the many enemies who wanted to kill him. After all of these suggestions by the classical commentators, Amos Hakham concludes that the connection between the superscription and body of the psalm remains difficult to understand.

Two additional approaches are available based on the principles discussed in the introductory chapter regarding superscriptions in the book of Psalms. *Le-David* (of David) does not necessarily mean that David composed this psalm. It may be that at the dedication of either the First or Second Temple, someone composed this psalm in David's honor. The mortal danger described in the psalm refers to the enemies of Israel.

Alternatively, Nahum Sarna suggests that this psalm could have been composed for one reason and then later applied to the dedication of the Second Temple. The original psalmist could have composed this psalm to thank God for saving him from illness, enemies, or both. Or, he could have composed it for others to use liturgically in these contexts. Later at the dedication of the Second Temple, the Temple builders allegorized the illness of this psalm to refer to Israel's exile. The original intent of the psalm is thus transformed into a national context, thanking God for returning the Jews to Israel and allowing them to rebuild the Temple. A regular "psalm of David" could grow into "a song for the dedication of the House."[5]

If Sarna is correct, the original author of the psalm intended one meaning, while someone at the dedication of the Second Temple gave it a new meaning, and added to the superscription to accommodate the new applied meaning. This is similar to Radak's understanding of Psalm 3, which began as a prayer from distress and later was incorporated into the Temple liturgy as a psalm of gratitude. Psalms sometimes grew or transformed in meaning through the biblical period.

PSALM 51

For the leader. A psalm of David, when Nathan the prophet came to him after he had come to Bathsheba. Have mercy upon me, O God, as befits Your faithfulness; in keeping with Your abundant compassion, blot out my transgressions. Wash me thoroughly of my iniquity, and purify me of my sin…

You do not want me to bring sacrifices; You do not desire burnt offerings; true sacrifice to God is a contrite spirit; God, You will not despise a contrite and crushed heart. May it please You to make Zion prosper; rebuild the walls of Jerusalem. Then You will want sacrifices offered in righteousness, burnt and whole offerings; then bulls will be offered on Your altar.

In Psalm 51, David expresses remorse and repentance following the Bathsheba affair. He pleads with God to restore their relationship, and desires to rebuild his soul after this terrible sin. In the context of a personal introspection, the psalm's final two verses seem out of place. The plea for the building of Jerusalem's walls seems to refer to the period after the destruction of the First Temple in 586 BCE, some four centuries after David. Rashi suggests that after praying for personal atonement, David prayed for the Temple to be built by Solomon. However, this view is difficult because the psalmist prays for the building of the walls of Jerusalem, not the Temple. More importantly, people were permitted to offer sacrifices on other shrines (*bamot*) during David's time, whereas the final two verses of this psalm suggest that people could not offer them on God's altar, referring to the one in the Temple.

Ibn Ezra quotes a Spanish rabbi who maintained that these two verses were added at the time of the destruction of the First Temple. In this reading, later writers drew inspiration from David's prayer for forgiveness after the Bathsheba episode and pleaded to God: "Please forgive us as You forgave David." The psalm took on a national meaning, similar to Sarna's reading of Psalm 30 discussed above. In Psalm 30, the prayer transformed in meaning at a later period, and words were added to the superscription to reflect that transition. In the case of Psalm 51, two new verses were appended to transform its meaning from the sin and repentance of an individual to that of the nation.

We have seen how different psalms may have transformed in intent within the biblical period: from distress to gratitude, from the individual to national, from personal to liturgical. More importantly, reciting the psalms transforms those who pray. By turning to God, we no longer are the same as before we prayed as we draw closer to a relationship with God. Thus, the structure and thematic development of these psalms reflect the religious growth of the individual through prayer.

NOTES

1. The term "Selah" appears 71 times in Psalms, distributed among 39 psalms. The psalm in Habakkuk 3 is the only usage of "Selah" outside of Psalms. Some midrashic traditions and later commentators interpret the word to mean "forever." Ibn Ezra objects to this interpretation, since there are instances where the word cannot mean forever, such as the one-time historical reference to the waters of Meribah in the Torah: "In distress you called and I rescued you; I answered you from the secret place of thunder I tested you at the waters of Meribah. Selah" (Psalm 81:8). Ibn Ezra interprets "Selah" as a synonym to "Amen." Rabbi Samson Raphael Hirsch and Malbim interpret the word as signifying the end of a section. Offering perhaps the most likely explanation, Radak and Amos Hakham suggest that "Selah" is a musical notation, like many other Psalms-specific terms that we no longer understand.
2. Amos Hakham, *Da'at Mikra: Psalms* vol. 1 (Hebrew) (Jerusalem: Mossad HaRav Kook, 1979), p. 59.
3. *Iyyunim BeMizmorei Tehillim* (Tel Aviv: Yediot Aharonot, 2012), pp. 24–37.
4. Hakham, *Da'at Mikra: Psalms* vol. 1, p. 222.
5. Nahum M. Sarna, *On the Book of Psalms: Exploring the Prayers of Ancient Israel* (New York: Schocken Books, 1993), pp. 148–150. See also Elhanan Samet, *Iyyunim BeMizmorei Tehillim*, pp. 107–108; Feivel Meltzer, *Penei Sefer Tehillim* (Jerusalem: Mossad HaRav Kook, 1982), p. 73.

Psalms 9–10:
Two Psalms or One?

PSALM 9

For the leader; *almuth labben*.¹ A psalm of David. I will praise You, Lord, with all my heart; I will tell all Your wonders. I will rejoice and exult in You, singing a hymn to Your name, O Most High. When my enemies retreat, they stumble to their doom at Your presence. For You uphold my right and claim, enthroned as righteous judge. You blast the nations; You destroy the wicked; You blot out their name forever. The enemy is no more – ruins everlasting; You have torn down their cities; their very names are lost. But the Lord abides forever; He has set up His throne for judgment; it is He who judges the world with righteousness, rules the peoples with equity. The Lord is a haven for the oppressed, a haven in times of trouble. Those who know Your name trust You, for You do not abandon those who turn to You, O Lord. Sing a hymn to the Lord, who reigns in Zion; declare His deeds among the peoples. For He does not ignore the cry of the afflicted; He who requites bloodshed is mindful of them.

 Have mercy on me, O Lord; see my affliction at the hands of my foes, You who lift me from the gates of death, so that in the gates of Fair Zion I might tell all Your praise, I might exult

---

A modified version of this essay is forthcoming in a volume on the book of Psalms by Yeshiva University Press.

in Your deliverance. The nations sink in the pit they have made; their own foot is caught in the net they have hidden. The Lord has made Himself known: He works judgment; the wicked man is snared by his own devices. *Higgaion.* Selah. Let the wicked be in Sheol, all the nations who ignore God! Not always shall the needy be ignored, nor the hope of the afflicted forever lost. Rise, O Lord! Let not men have power; let the nations be judged in Your presence. Strike fear into them, O Lord; let the nations know they are only men. Selah.

Psalm 9 is fairly simple to outline: Verses 2–13 express praise and gratitude to God for winning a war. God is just, defeats Israel's enemies, and deserves praise for hearing the prayers of the humble. Verses 14–21 petition God for salvation from enemies (with the exception of verses 16–17, which sound like praise and thanksgiving).

Although that outline is straightforward, it immediately presents a conceptual difficulty. If the first half of the psalm thanks God for salvation, then why would the psalm petition God for salvation after that? Psalm 9 moves in the opposite direction from Psalms 3, 6, 13, 20, and many others, where the order makes more sense: first a petition for salvation, then an expression of greater confidence in God's salvation.

Amos Hakham[2] offers three approaches to understanding the relationship between the two sections:

- The psalm may be recited in times of trouble. The gratitude at the outset of the psalm functions as a vow: If God will save us, we will thank God.
- The psalm expresses praise/gratitude for salvation that already has occurred. The petition in the second half is a flashback to the prayers he said during distress. This flashback magnifies the current praise, expressing gratitude over the fact that he had prayed while in trouble, and now has been saved.
- The psalm expresses gratitude for past salvations, and the psalmist then prays for salvation from the current danger. "As You have saved me in the past, please save me now."

We may uphold all three readings rather than choosing one, since the book of Psalms was written for all occasions. This psalm may be used by someone currently in distress or by someone who already has been saved from distress. Psalms do not need to move in a linear progression.

Is there a connection between Psalms 9 and 10?
Let us now consider Psalm 10:

> Why, O Lord, do You stand aloof, heedless in times of trouble? The wicked in his arrogance hounds the lowly – may they be caught in the schemes they devise! The wicked crows about his unbridled lusts; the grasping man reviles and scorns the Lord. The wicked, arrogant as he is, in all his scheming [thinks], "He does not call to account; God does not care." His ways prosper at all times; Your judgments are far beyond him; he snorts at all his foes. He thinks, "I shall not be shaken, through all time never be in trouble." His mouth is full of oaths, deceit, and fraud; mischief and evil are under his tongue. He lurks in outlying places; from a covert he slays the innocent; his eyes spy out the hapless. He waits in a covert like a lion in his lair; waits to seize the lowly; he seizes the lowly as he pulls his net shut; he stoops, he crouches, and the hapless fall prey to his might. He thinks, "God is not mindful, He hides His face, He never looks."
>
> Rise, O Lord! Strike at him, O God! Do not forget the lowly. Why should the wicked man scorn God, thinking You do not call to account? You do look! You take note of mischief and vexation! To requite is in Your power. To You the hapless can entrust himself; You have ever been the orphan's help. O break the power of the wicked and evil man, so that when You look for his wickedness You will find it no more. The Lord is king for ever and ever; the nations will perish from His land. You will listen to the entreaty of the lowly, O Lord, You will make their hearts firm; You will incline Your ear to champion the

orphan and the downtrodden, that men who are of the earth tyrannize no more.

If we were to open a scroll containing the Psalms, how would we know how many units are in the book? Aside from superscriptions and closing formulas, there is often no definite way to demarcate sections. Consequently, different traditions divide the psalms in various ways. The Greek Septuagint has 150 psalms, like the Masoretic Text, but it has different divisions. For example, it reads Psalms 9–10 as one unit, 114–115 are one unit, and it divides 116 and 147 into two psalms each.[3] Some rabbinic traditions divide our book into 147 psalms.[4] Meiri had 151 psalms in his version.

We must attempt to define the boundaries of each psalm so that we may interpret the psalm as a complete unit. Adopting the view of several contemporary scholars, Rabbi Avia HaCohen[5] suggests that Psalms 9–10 may in fact be one psalm that should be learned as a single unit. Rabbi Hacohen observes that there is no superscription on Psalm 10, which is unusual in the first book of psalms (1–41). Only Psalms 1, 2, 10, and 33 begin without an introductory formula. Additionally, the Septuagint considers Psalms 9–10 as one psalm, so an ancient Jewish tradition supports this reading.

Most significantly, there may be an acrostic over (generally) alternating verses (like in Psalm 37). Several other acrostic psalms are missing one or two letters. Psalm 9 covers from *aleph* until *kaf*, and then Psalm 10 picks up with *lamed*.

However, while only *daled* is missing from the acrostic in Psalm 9, the acrostic completely vanishes after the opening *lamed* in Psalm 10. It resumes only at 10:12, with *kof, resh, shin, tav*. Why are so many letters missing from the acrostic? Rabbi Hacohen quotes a common secular academic response, that Psalms 9–10 likely were originally one psalm with a complete acrostic. However, the text is now hopelessly corrupt from scribal errors. Although this approach is always possible, it is overly facile and alternatives should be explored.

Rabbi Hacohen proposes an answer by considering the structure of a larger psalm that encompasses Psalms 9–10:

- 9:2–13 gratitude for salvation from enemies.
- 9:14–21 petition for salvation from enemies.
- 10:1–11 bitter protest that God has not saved Israel from their enemies.
- 10:12–18 petition for salvation from enemies.

Rabbi Hacohen observes that a poet generally uses acrostics to express completeness and order. Psalm 9 is an expression of faith in God's justice, but then Psalm 10 explodes with a protest against God's injustice: how come God isn't saving us now? The psalmist then regains his composure and returns to a petition for salvation in 10:12–18. Rabbi Hacohen submits that the content of the psalms explains precisely why the acrostic breaks down after the *lamed* at the beginning of Psalm 10. When the psalmist protests, he loses his sense of order and fairness. He expresses this despair poetically by suspending the acrostic structure. Once the psalmist grounds himself at the end by returning to petition, the acrostic resumes.

Rabbi Hacohen concludes his analysis by noting that acrostic poetry does not constrain poets by forcing them to adhere to an artificial structure. Rather, it is a poetic tool to express emotions and ideas. In this remarkable case, the psalmist suspends an acrostic to convey a loss of order. When he regains his confidence in God's salvation, order returns to his world.

ACROSTICS IN PSALMS[6]

Book	Psalm	Format	Missing Letter(s)	Missing Letter Count	Letter Added To End	Total Letters
1	9/10	Every other verse on average	ד, מ, נ, ס, ע, פ, צ	7	-	15
1	25	Every verse	ב, ו, ק	2–3	פ	20+1=21
1	34	Every verse	ו	1	פ	21+1=22
1	37	Every other verse on average	ע	1	-	21
5	111	Every half-verse	Complete	0	-	22
5	112	Every half-verse	Complete	0	-	22
5	119	Eight verses each	Complete	0	-	22
5	145	Every verse	נ	1	-	21

NOTES

1. The meaning of these words is uncertain.
2. Amos Hakham, *Da'at Mikra: Psalms* vol. 1 (Hebrew) (Jerusalem: Mossad HaRav Kook, 1979), p. 40.
3. The Septuagint also has a 151st psalm, noting that it is "outside the number." Some of the Dead Sea Scrolls have this psalm in Hebrew form.
4. JT *Shabbat* 16:1; *Midrash Psalms* 22:4. This tradition carried into the medieval period as well. Tosafot, *Pesahim* 117a, s.v. *she-omedim*, Rabbi Yaakov Baal HaTurim (on Genesis 47:28), and Rabbi Yosef Hayyun (introduction, p. 32 in Kapah edition) had 147 psalms.
5. Avia Hacohen, *Tefillah le-El Hai: The Journey of the Soul and the Spirit of the Song in the Book of Psalms* (Hebrew) (En Tzurim: Yeshivat HaKibbutz HaDati, 2007), pp. 15–31.
6. Chart from Ronald Benun, "Evil and the Disruption of Order: A Structural Analysis of the Acrostics in the First Book of Psalms," *Journal of Hebrew Scriptures* 6.5 (2006).

Psalms 14–53: Redundant Psalms?

PSALM 14

For the leader. Of David. The benighted man [*naval*] thinks, "God does not care." Man's deeds are corrupt and loathsome; no one does good. The Lord looks down from heaven on mankind to find a man of understanding, a man mindful of God. All have turned bad, altogether foul; there is none who does good, not even one. Are they so witless, all those evildoers, who devour my people as they devour food, and do not invoke the Lord? There they will be seized with fright, for God is present in the circle of the righteous. You may set at naught the counsel of the lowly, but the Lord is his refuge. O that the deliverance of Israel might come from Zion! When the Lord restores the fortunes of His people, Jacob will exult, Israel will rejoice.

Psalm 14 is brief and straightforward. The world's unfairness leads wicked individuals to abandon faith in divine providence, thereby encouraging them to perform more evil deeds. There is a transition in the middle of the psalm, as the psalmist expresses shock that wicked people do not realize that God sees everything. The psalm concludes with an expression of hope that God will save Israel.

A modified version of this essay is forthcoming in a volume on the book of Psalms by Yeshiva University Press.

Surprisingly, this psalm is repeated almost verbatim in Psalm 53:

> For the leader; on *mahalath*. A *maskil* of David. The benighted man thinks, "God does not care." Man's wrongdoing is corrupt and loathsome; no one does good. God looks down from heaven on mankind to find a man of understanding, a man mindful of God. Everyone is dross, altogether foul; there is none who does good, not even one. Are they so witless, those evildoers, who devour my people as they devour food, and do not invoke God? There they will be seized with fright – never was there such a fright – for God has scattered the bones of your besiegers; you have put them to shame, for God has rejected them. O that the deliverance of Israel might come from Zion! When God restores the fortunes of His people, Jacob will exult, Israel will rejoice.

Psalms 42–83 tend to favor God's Name *Elokim* over the Tetragrammaton (210 vs. 45 in these psalms), whereas the other psalms favor the Tetragrammaton to *Elokim* (584 vs. 94). This statistic readily explains the difference between these two names of God in the two psalms. Other than this, however, there are only a few minor variations. They are essentially the same psalm.[1]

Amos Hakham[2] often stresses that we must attempt to understand each psalm on its own terms, rather than simply assuming that the same verses in two different places must have the identical meaning. For example, Psalm 108 contains many of the verses from Psalms 57 and 60 (108:2–6~57:8–12; 108:7–14~60:7–14).[3] We should not immediately assume that the verses have the identical meaning in each case, since together the verses in Psalm 108 form a new composition.

There are several repetitions of blocks of verses in other psalms. For example, 70:2–6 dovetails 40:14–18, and 71:1–3 resembles 31:2–4. There also are two important examples of blocks of verses in Psalms appearing in other biblical books. The lengthy prayer sung as David brought the Ark to Jerusalem (I Chronicles 16:8–36) parallels verses from three different psalms (105:1–15; 96:1–13; 106:1, 47–48).[4] David's hymn of salvation from his enemies appears with minor variations in II Samuel 22 and Psalm 18.[5] In this instance, the fact that they are included in different books does not present any difficulties. One psalm is an appendix to David's life, and therefore belongs in the book of Samuel, and the other is a stand-alone psalm that fits naturally into the book of Psalms. There are no other instances other than Psalms 14 and 53 where an entire psalm appears twice as a complete unit within the book of Psalms itself. They appear to be redundant.

To eliminate the ostensible redundancy, several commentators submit that each psalm must refer to a different historical enemy of Israel.

- Rashi and Meiri suggest that 14 refers to Nebuchanezzar, whereas 53 refers to Titus (cf. *Gittin* 56b). The two psalms thereby reflect the destroyers of the two Temples in Jerusalem.
- Radak proposes that 14 refers to Nebuchadnezzar, and 53 refers to pre-Messianic enemies of Israel. Rashi, Radak, and Meiri all assume that David had prophetic foreknowledge of enemies who lived long after David's lifetime.
- Rabbi Yeshayah of Trani keeps both references within the biblical period. 14 refers to Nebuchadnezzar while 53 refers to the Assyrian tyrant, Sennacherib. Assuming David is still the author, the psalms likewise reflect prophetic foreknowledge.
- Malbim also associates both psalms with events in the biblical period. David composed 14 in reference to his own enemies, and the people living in Sennacherib's time updated the psalm with minor variations to suit their needs for Psalm 53. In this reading, there is no prophetic foreknowledge.

The common denominator of the aforementioned interpretations is that the two psalms are not redundant. Each refers to a different enemy of Israel.

Rabbi Yaakov Medan proposes a different interpretation.[6] The "benighted one" (*naval*) in Psalm 14 refers to the generic evildoer, rather than a specific historical figure. Psalm 53, in contrast, refers to the obnoxious character Nabal in I Samuel 25. Nabal rudely refused to feed David and his men when David was a refugee fleeing from Saul.

To adduce support for this position, Rabbi Medan observes that Psalm 14 is surrounded by other psalms pertaining to righteous and wicked behavior (12, 15). Therefore, one may interpret *naval* as referring to the general wicked person. In contrast, Psalm 53 is surrounded by several psalms with historical-specific superscriptions related to David's life. Psalm 51 pertains to David's repentance after the sin with Bathsheba. Psalm 52 relates to Saul's wicked courtier Doeg, and Psalm 54 relates to the wicked Ziphites who turned David in to Saul. Although we cannot definitively rely on surrounding psalms for interpreting the content of a given psalm (see Ibn Ezra on 3:1), we may assume that *some* wisdom underlies the editorial order of the psalms.

Rabbi Medan observes further that the Targum on Psalms[7] appears to support his reading, as well. On 14:1, it renders the introduction, *amar shatya be-levavei*, "the fool says in his heart." On 53:1, in contrast, it renders the introduction, *amar Naval be-libbei*, "Nabal says in his heart."

Rabbi Medan's contextual reading of the two psalms, coupled with the Targum's apparent support, initially sounds appealing. However, since all the classical commentators struggled to identify the different subjects of the two psalms to eliminate the apparent redundancy, one may ask: Why did none of them think of identifying one of the *naval*s with David's contemporary Nabal? The answer appears fairly clear: 53:5 reads, "Are they so witless, those evildoers, who devour my people as they devour food, and do not invoke God?" (cf. similar in 14:4). People "who devour my people" are Israel's mortal enemies, and not a repulsive individual who refused a meal to David and his men. The psalm concludes with a prayer that God restore Israel's fortunes: "O that the deliverance of Israel might come from Zion! When God restores the fortunes of His people, Jacob will exult, Israel will rejoice" (53:7, cf. 14:7). This prayer suggests a recovery from national catastrophe. Sennacherib, Nebuchadnezzar, Titus, pre-Messianic invaders, or generic enemies, all fit this description. The boorish Nabal does not. Rabbi Medan's interpretation does not appear to solve the problem of redundancy.

For that matter, the aforementioned identifications of the *naval* with historical figures are difficult to support as *peshat* of the psalms, which seem to be general references to wicked enemies of Israel (Ibn Ezra, Hakham). Both psalms appear to mean essentially the same thing.

At this point, it is worth remembering that Psalm 14 appears in book one of Psalms (Psalms 1–41), and Psalm 53 is in book 2 (Psalms 42–72). While they both now are in what we call the book of Psalms, each psalm likely made its way into a separate collection, and therefore they are not redundant. This phenomenon is similar to the duplicate psalms of II Samuel 22 and Psalm 18, discussed above.

NOTES

1. For a survey of the variations between Psalms 14 and 53, see Feivel Meltzer, *Penei Sefer Tehillim* (Jerusalem: Mossad HaRav Kook, 1982), pp. 131–134.
2. E.g., *Da'at Mikra: Tehillim*, pp. 314, 421.
3. Radak and Meiri (on 108:1) are unsure why psalm 108 repeats so much material from psalms 57 and 60. They submit that perhaps 57 and 60 are about David, whereas 108 refers to the messianic era. Alternatively, Rabbi Yosef Hayyun (on 108:1) suggests that perhaps God saved David after his prayers in 57 (from Saul) and 60 (from Edom and other nations), and later combined these ideas into 108 to thank God for all these salvations together.
4. Radak (on 105:1) maintains that the version in Chronicles is the original. When David later composed psalms, he divided this prayer into two units that appear in Psalms 105 and 96. In contrast, Meiri (on 105:1) argues that David first composed the units that appear in the book of Psalms. When David moved the Ark (in 1 Chronicles 16), he combined these units into a larger hymn for the occasion.
5. Radak and Amos Hakham do not think that the minor variations between the versions in Samuel and Psalms are significant. Abarbanel and Malbim do consider the variations as significant. Abarbanel (on II Samuel 22) counts 74 discrepancies, and argues that David updated and clarified the psalm from the version in Samuel, and then added it to the book of Psalms. He considers the Samuel version to be praise for past salvations, whereas Psalm 18 is a prayer for future salvation.
6. Yaakov Medan, "The Benighted One Says in His Heart" (Hebrew), *Megadim* 4 (1988), pp. 23–54.
7. Rashi on *Megillah* 21b says that there is no Targum on Psalms, so he evidently was unaware of this Targum. Tosafot, who were aware of this Targum, maintain that it is tannaitic, but not from Rabbi Yonatan ben Uzziel. See also *Megillah* 3a, where Rabbi Yonatan ben Uzziel's Targum of the Holy Writings (Ketuvim) were hidden, but Tosafot *ad loc.* observe that someone else did compose Targum on the Ketuvim.

Psalm 19:
Nature and Torah

On its surface, Psalm 19 is straightforward. Verses 2–7 proclaim that God's glory is revealed through nature. Verses 8–15 then praise God's Torah and its effects on people. The relationship between the sections of the psalm has elicited various responses by commentators throughout the ages. How one connects them reflects and affects one's religious outlook in significant ways. In this essay we explore several facets of interpretation.

CONNECTING THE TWO HALVES OF THE PSALM

Rabbi Elhanan Samet[1] divides the first half of the psalm into two subsections: the heavens' declaration of God's glory (2–5a), and the daily activity of the sun (5b–7):

> For the leader. A psalm of David. The heavens declare the glory of God, the sky proclaims His handiwork. Day to day makes utterance, night to night speaks out. There is no utterance, there are no words, whose sound goes unheard. Their voice carries throughout the earth, their words to the end of the world.

This essay is adapted from my article, "Perspectives on Psalm 19," in *The Keys to the Palace: Essays Exploring the Religious Value of Reading the Bible* (New York: Kodesh Press, 2017), pp. 249–258.

Heavens speak, but without words. Consequently, we must pay special attention to hear the praises that the heavens utter. Rabbi Samet quotes from the Talmud: "Were it not for the sound of the tumult of Rome, the sound of the revolution of the sun would be heard" (*Yoma* 20b). It is possible to drown out the sounds of God's glory with too much emphasis on mundane existence. The opening verses of this psalm describe the glory of God manifest throughout the cosmos, and how people must direct their attentiveness in order to hear the beauty of nature and how it glorifies God.

The psalmist then praises the sun for its joyful obedience of God's command. It perfectly fulfills its role to illuminate:

> He placed in them a tent for the sun, who is like a groom coming forth from the chamber, like a hero, eager to run his course. His rising-place is at one end of heaven, and his circuit reaches the other; nothing escapes his heat.

The section concludes *ve-en nistar me-hamato*, translated by several commentators as "nothing escapes its heat." Rabbi Samet observes that everything else describing the sun is positive. He therefore adopts the reading of Rabbi Samson Raphael Hirsch, who explains that *hamato* means God's sun (*hamah* is another Hebrew word for sun[2]) and not the sun's heat. No place on earth is hidden from the sun's light. Alternatively, Amos Hakham explains that nobody can hide from the sun's warmth and rays, which likewise conveys a positive tone.[3]

Moving to the second half of the psalm, verses 8–11 praise the Torah, its commandments, and its influence on people. Verses 12–14 are then a prayer to God to save the psalmist from sin, and verse 15 concludes with a prayer that the psalmist's words should be acceptable to God:

> The teaching of the Lord is perfect, renewing life; the decrees of the Lord are enduring, making the simple wise; The precepts of the Lord are just, rejoicing the heart; the instruction of the Lord is lucid, making the eyes light up. The fear of the Lord is pure, abiding forever; the judgments of the Lord are true,

righteous altogether, more desirable than gold, than much fine gold; sweeter than honey, than drippings of the comb. Your servant pays them heed; in obeying them there is much reward. Who can be aware of errors? Clear me of unperceived guilt, and from willful sins keep Your servant; let them not dominate me; then shall I be blameless and clear of grave offense. May the words of my mouth and the prayer of my heart be acceptable to You, O Lord, my Rock and my Redeemer.

Commentators adopt different strategies for linking the two halves of our psalm. Some see a similarity between the two halves. Within those who see the two halves as parallel, there is discussion whether the religious values of nature and Torah are different but equal ways of approaching God, or whether the psalm presents the Torah as a superior means of developing a relationship with God. Rashi (first view) and Amos Hakham[4] parallel the two halves: just as the sun illuminates, so does the Torah. Similarly, Radak (second view) argues that just as the sun is necessary for physical existence, the Torah is vital for the nourishment of our souls. Ibn Ezra, Radak (first view), and Meiri view the Torah as superior to nature: we find testimony to God's greatness in nature, and the Torah is even greater testimony.

Rabbi Samson Raphael Hirsch suggests that the study of nature teaches any thoughtful person that there is a God. However, heavens and earth cannot provide people with answers to the question of why we should praise God, or why we should recognize God as Master. Nature cannot answer the question of what people should do with their free will. The contemplation of nature will never teach us our purpose in this world. It is only Torah that can shape people in accordance with God's will.

Other commentators view the two halves of the psalm as contrasting. Rashi (second view) interprets the final expression in the first half, *ve-en nistar me-hamato*, "nothing escapes his heat" (v. 7), as negative. The sun can burn, whereas the Torah heals and restores the soul. A more dramatic contrasting approach is found in Rabbenu Bahya ben Asher's *Kad ha-Kemah* in his entry on "Torah." Rabbenu

Bahya quotes Psalm 19:8–10, and gives a detailed analysis of how each aspect of Torah is superior to some aspect of the sun. For example, one looking directly at the sun can be blinded, but the Torah brightens our eyes. The sun shines only during the day, whereas the Torah perpetually illuminates. As noted above, Amos Hakham and Rabbi Samet disagree with the negative reading of *ve-en nistar me-hamato*. The first half of the psalm appears entirely positive in its praise of all nature, including the sun.

Rabbi Samet explains that the heavens attest to God's greatness. The sun is the ideal model of the heavenly realm, serving God with perfection and enthusiasm. This paradigm is not identical to the human realm. The psalmist longs to achieve the sun's perfection and enthusiasm in serving God, but recognizes that as a human being he cannot be perfect. People are liable to error, and sometimes those errors are hidden (*nistarot*) even from themselves. In contrast, nothing is hidden (*nistar*) from the sun's light.[5] The sun therefore rejoices like a bridegroom, whereas the religious person worries. The parallel between the two halves of the psalm is that God created perfection in nature, and in the Torah. The religious individual considers the sun as a role model in serving God, and prays that he will avoid error in the effort to likewise attain perfection in serving God through the Torah.

Whereas the aforementioned medieval commentators do not interpret this psalm in this manner, *Sifrei Deuteronomy* 306 explicitly expresses this idea:

> "Give ear, O heavens, and I will speak" (Deuteronomy 32:1) – The Holy One, blessed be He, said to Moses: Say to Israel: Look into the heavens that I created to serve you. Have they perhaps changed their ways? Did perhaps the sphere of the sun say: I shall not rise in the east and illuminate the entire world? Rather as it is stated, "The sun also rises, and the sun goes down" (Ecclesiastes 1:5). And what is more, it is happy to do My will, as it is stated: "And it is like a bridegroom coming out of his chamber" (Psalm 19:6). Surely there is an *a fortiori* argument: If they who do not act for reward nor for loss – if

they merit they do not receive reward, and if they sin they do receive punishment – and do not have compassion for their sons and daughters – if they do not change their ways, then you, who if you merit you receive reward, and if you sin you receive punishment, and you have compassion for your sons and for your daughters, all the more so you must not change your ways.

In this Midrash, the sun is a model for humanity. As the sun perfectly fulfills God's will constantly, so too people should strive to fulfill God's will as well. When people use their free will properly in the service of God, humanity is in harmony with the cosmos.

BREAKING THE PSALM INTO THREE PARTS

J. Ross Wagner and Philip Nel offer additional insight into Psalm 19 by dividing it into three sections rather than two.[6] Wagner observes that verses 2–7 speak about nature as objectively awesome, and do not refer to people. These verses refer to God as *El*, referring to God's capacity as the Creator of the cosmos. Verses 8–11 bring God closer to people, exulting in how God's Torah benefits people. In these verses, the psalmist does not address God directly, but talks about Him using God's name Y-H-V-H, implying a more personal, intimate, covenantal relationship. Verses 12–15 bring God still closer, as the psalmist directly addresses God for the first time. The psalm's seventh and final reference to God's personal name (v. 15) is the only time that the psalmist addresses God by name. The concluding address to God as *Tzuri ve-Go'ali*, "my Rock and my Redeemer," reflects God's intimate relationship with the psalmist. Thus, the psalmist is awed by the cosmos, then by the Torah, and then he internalizes these means to shape and transform his own religious life. The psalmist wants to take his place in this infinite and eternal order in perfect service to God.

Adopting a different approach that also divides the psalm into three sections, Philip Nel argues that the cosmos (2–7) and Torah (8–11) are both perfect, whereas people are not (12–14). Instead of remaining mute, however, people can and should speak God's praises and meditate on God's greatness (15). Though we are imperfect, when we pray, we join nature and the Torah in glorifying God.

COMBINING TORAH AND SCIENCE

Rabbi Norman Lamm discusses an apparent conflict within Rambam's writings.[7] Rambam writes that one attains love of God through contemplating nature (*Hilkhot Yesodei ha-Torah* 2:2; see also *Guide of the Perplexed* 3:28 and 3:52). However, in his *Sefer ha-Mitzvot*, Rambam includes both mitzvah observance and contemplation of nature as means to attaining love of God (positive commandment 3). Why is Rambam inconsistent?

Rabbi Lamm adopts an approach common in Rambam scholarship, and distinguishes between Rambam's writing for the masses and the intellectual elite. The masses love God through observance of the Torah's commandments, whereas the philosophical elite love God through nature. The *Guide* is elitist, whereas *Sefer ha-Mitzvot* was written as a popular work. What about the *Mishneh Torah*, a work similarly intended for everyone? Rabbi Lamm answers that its opening chapters are philosophical, and therefore can be understood properly only by an exclusive elite.

One may question this explanation. Even the simplest soul can be religiously moved and overwhelmed by the cosmos. Several psalms – Psalm 19 included – express that sentiment. Perhaps the discrepancy in Rambam's writings has more to do with the context of each book. *Sefer ha-Mitzvot* teaches how Jews develop a love of God – through the Torah's commandments and through the contemplation of nature. In contrast, the opening chapters in *Mishneh Torah* and the *Guide* focus on how any religious person attains the love and fear of God. Therefore, they highlight the universal aspects of God's glory in nature.

In his book *Torah Umadda*,[8] Rabbi Lamm quotes the Mishnah in *Avot* 3:7: "Rabbi Yaakov used to say: One who is studying Torah as he walks by the way, and who interrupts his studies to say, 'How beautiful is this tree,' or 'how beautiful is this furrow,' it is as though he is guilty with his life." Rabbi Lamm adopts Rashi's interpretation of the Mishnah: nature certainly helps us appreciate God, but the Torah is God's revealed word and therefore it has religious primacy. This interpretation of the Mishnah dovetails with the comments of Ibn Ezra, Radak (first view), and Meiri on Psalm 19 that we considered earlier, who view the Torah as superior to nature.

Rabbi Marc D. Angel pointed out to me an alternate interpretation of the Mishnah in *Avot*. One who views nature as an *interruption* from Torah errs. One who perceives nature as part of a Torah worldview has a proper religious understanding. As Psalm 19 teaches, Torah and nature are different manifestations of God's voice. Because they are different, the psalm separates them into two categories. However, they are two means of hearing God's voice, and they work together in harmony. This interpretation is in line with Rashi (first view), Radak (second view), and Amos Hakham, who see the Torah and nature as parallel means of connecting to God in Psalm 19.

Amos Hakham observes that the blessings before the *Shema* follow this pattern, as well. The first blessing praises God as the Creator of the cosmos, whereas the second focuses on Israel's intimate personal relationship with God. Armed with both aspects, we accept the yoke of Heaven by reciting the *Shema*.[9]

Psalm 19 teaches that the Torah and nature are different manifestations of God's voice. Concurrently, they are two means of hearing God's voice that work together in harmony. The job of humanity is to perceive God's glory in nature and the Torah, and speak out God's praises. In this manner, all creation harmoniously unites in the service of God.

NOTES

1. Elhanan Samet, *Iyyunim be-Mizmorei Tehillim* (Hebrew) (Tel Aviv: Yediot Aharonot, 2012), pp. 41–69.
2. See Isaiah 24:23; 30:26; Job 30:28; Song of Songs 6:10.
3. Amos Hakham, *Da'at Mikra: Psalms* vol. 1 (Hebrew) (Jerusalem: Mosad HaRav Kook, 1979), p. 99.
4. Ibid., p. 102.
5. In a similar vein, C.S. Lewis suggests that the psalmist feels that one cannot hide from the searching light of the sun, nor can one hide one's soul from the all-encompassing light of the Torah (*Reflections on the Psalms: The Celebrated Musings on One of the Most Intriguing Books of the Bible* [Boston: Mariner Books, 2012 edition of the 1958 publication]), p. 64.
6. J. Ross Wagner, "From the Heavens to the Heart: The Dynamics of Psalm 19 as Prayer," *Catholic Biblical Quarterly* 61 (1999), pp. 245–261; Philip Nel, "Psalm 19: The Unbearable Lightness of Perfection," *Journal of Northwest Semitic Languages* 30 (2004), pp. 103–117.
7. "Maimonides on the Love of God," *Maimonidean Studies* 3 (1992–1993), pp. 131–142.
8. *Torah Umadda: The Encounter of Religious Learning and Worldly Knowledge in the Jewish Tradition* (Lanham, MD: Rowman and Littlefield, 2004), pp. 146–147.
9. Ibid., pp. 102–103.

Psalms 18, 57, 59, 63, 142:
David and Saul in the Psalms

INTRODUCTION

When Saul was afflicted with his evil spirit, he hurled spears at David, attempted to set his children Jonathan and Michal against him, and eventually pursued David with the army. He did all this although David had killed Goliath, had served as Saul's arms-bearer and musician, and had been an extremely devoted subject.

No less remarkable than Saul's violent behavior towards David, however, is David's persistent love and compassion for Saul. The first time David had the chance to kill Saul, David's men viewed the opportunity as a divine blessing. David, however, emphatically rejected his men's suggestion:

> David's men said to him, "This is the day of which the Lord said to you, 'I will deliver your enemy into your hands; you can do with him as you please.'" David went and stealthily cut off the corner of Saul's cloak. But afterward David reproached himself for cutting off the corner of Saul's cloak. He said to his men "The Lord forbid that I should do such a thing to my lord – the Lord's anointed – that I should raise my hand against him; for

---

This essay is adapted from my article, "Why Didn't He Do It? An Analysis of Why David Did Not Kill Saul," in *Through an Opaque Lens*, revised second edition (New York: Kodesh Press, 2013), pp. 135–148.

he is the Lord's anointed." David rebuked his men and did not permit them to attack Saul (I Samuel 24:5–8).

David settled for cutting off the corner of Saul's coat, and later regretted having done even this act against God's anointed.

Two chapters later, David again was presented with an opportunity to kill Saul. Abishai wanted to deliver the fatal blow to Saul, but again David strongly opposed such an action:

> And Abishai said to David, "God has delivered your enemy into your hands today. Let me pin him to the ground with a single thrust of the spear. I will not have to strike him twice." But David said to Abishai, "Don't do him violence! No one can lay hands on the Lord's anointed with impunity" (I Samuel 26:8–9).

David expressed his loyalty to Saul most poignantly after the latter perished in battle. David promptly ordered the execution of the youth who claimed to have killed Saul (II Samuel 1:13–16). Similarly, David acted swiftly against the assassins of Saul's son, Ish-bosheth, demonstrating his loyalty to Saul and his family (II Samuel 4:9–12).

Even with our awareness of David's greatness and piety, it is difficult to imagine that he harbored no resentment towards Saul. Ralbag and Abarbanel (on I Samuel 24:5) suggest that in addition to his religious motivations, David did have a different motive for sparing the king: David knew that he was to succeed Saul as king of Israel. If he were to assassinate the first king, Saul, then perhaps someone else might decide to assassinate the second king, David. Ralbag and Abarbanel (on II Samuel 1:14) assert further that it was for the same reason that David ordered the youth who claimed to have killed Saul (II Samuel 1:2–10) executed – David wanted to make it clear that regicide is an unforgivable crime.[1] While affirming that David was motivated by piety, Ralbag and Abarbanel assert that his actions also included this more practical impetus for his exceptional restraint.

One's attitude towards David, not to mention one's outlook when studying biblical heroes in general, undoubtedly will affect whether one inclines towards the purer portrayal of David, or whether one incorporates the more utilitarian dimension suggested by Ralbag and Abarbanel.[2] Perhaps, however, we have a different tool in this instance, using a source which we have for no other biblical character: the Psalms. In this essay, we will consider the Psalms whose superscriptions associate them with the period of David fleeing Saul, and show how these Psalms may serve as a midrashic-intertextual window for understanding the narratives in the book of Samuel.

METHODOLOGICAL CONSIDERATIONS

There are at least seven Psalms where the superscription identifies a specific event during Saul's pursuit of David.

1. Psalm 18: For the leader. Of David, the servant of the Lord, who addressed the words of this song to the Lord after the Lord had saved him from the hands of all his enemies, and from the clutches of Saul.
2. Psalm 52: For the leader. A *maskil* of David, when Doeg the Edomite came and informed Saul, telling him, "David came to Abimelech's house."
3. Psalm 54: For the leader; with instrumental music. A *maskil* of David, when the Ziphites came and told Saul, "Know, David is hiding among us."
4. Psalm 57: For the leader; *al tashhet*. Of David. A *michtam*; when he fled from Saul into a cave.
5. Psalm 59: For the leader; *al tashhet*. Of David. A *michtam*; when Saul sent men to watch his house in order to put him to death.
6. Psalm 63: A psalm of David, when he was in the Wilderness of Judah.
7. Psalm 142: A *maskil* of David, while he was in the cave. A prayer.[3]

Although one might assume that the prayers expressed in these seven Psalms reflect David's feelings towards Saul and his men (with the exception of Psalm 52 which discusses Doeg, and Psalm 54 which criticizes the Ziphites), the matter is not so simple.

There are two methodological questions to address:

1. In these Psalms, was David praying exclusively for himself (and the Psalm later became canonized for others to use), or did David originally consider his prayers as a formula for others to use, regardless of what David was experiencing as he wrote them?
2. How close is the relationship between the body of a Psalm with its superscription? Must we assume that the entire Psalm reflects the event specified in the superscription, or is it possible that the Psalm speaks to broader circumstances, beyond any original event that may have inspired its composition?

A. *THE ORIGINAL INTENTION OF THE PSALMS*

The Talmud leaves the first issue unresolved:

> Our Rabbis have taught: all the songs and hymns which David said in the book of Psalms, Rabbi Eliezer says, he wrote them for himself. Rabbi Joshua says, he wrote them for the community. The Sages say, some are for the community, and others are for himself: those in the singular voice are for himself, while those in the plural voice are for the community (*Pesahim* 117a).

According to Rabbi Eliezer, David wrote all his Psalms as private prayers for himself. Later, these Psalms were publicized and canonized, and became accessible to others. Alternatively, Rabbi Joshua asserts that David originally composed the Psalms as communal prayers, and therefore he formulated them in more general terms so that they could be used for a wide array of occasions. The Sages adopt a middle position: those Psalms in the first-person singular were originally private prayers of David. Those Psalms in a plural voice were written originally as communal prayers. One midrashic view combines the various opinions: "Rabbi Yudan said in the name of Rabbi Judah: all that David said in his book was recited for himself, for all Israel, and for all times" (*Midrash Psalms* 18:1).

The five Psalms we will consider (18, 57, 59, 63 and 142) are all written in the first-person singular. According to both Rabbi Eliezer and the Sages, then, these Psalms were composed originally as private prayers, in which David pleaded to God to save him from Saul and his men. However, according to Rabbi Joshua, even these five Psalms were written initially as communal prayers, and do not pertain directly to David's personal life.

B. *THE RELATIONSHIP BETWEEN THE SUPERSCRIPTION AND THE BODY OF PSALMS*

Closely related to the issue of the original intent of a Psalm is whether the entire body of a Psalm must correspond to the introductory verse, or superscription. For example, Psalm 59 begins, "For the leader; *al tashhet*. Of David. A *michtam*; when Saul sent men to watch his house in order to put him to death." This superscription alludes to the narrative where Saul's daughter Michal helps her husband David escape Saul's men (1 Samuel 19:11–17). The beginning of Psalm 59 reads:

> Save me from my enemies, O my God; secure me against my assailants. Save me from evildoers, deliver me from murderers. For see, they lie in wait for me; fierce men plot against me for no offense of mine, for no transgression, O Lord; for no guilt of mine do they rush to array themselves against me. Look, rouse Yourself on my behalf! You, O Lord God of hosts, God of Israel, bestir Yourself to bring all nations to account; have no mercy on any treacherous villain (Psalm 59:2–6).

In general, the Psalms do not make references to specific events in David's life (with the exception of the superscriptions).[4] Were one to assume a direct relationship between a Psalm's specific superscription and its main body, then all references to "enemies" would be to Saul and his men. If, on the other hand, the main body of the Psalm may exceed the boundaries of its superscription, then one would not necessarily be able to associate every reference to David's feelings towards Saul and his men. Instead, we would conclude that this Psalm was composed as a general prayer that asks God to save oppressed people from their enemies.

This issue comes to the fore in verse six, "You, O Lord God of hosts, God of Israel, bestir Yourself to bring all nations to account; have no mercy on any treacherous villain." In this verse (and in verse 9), David refers to other nations. This reference supports those who contend that the body of a Psalm may refer to situations beyond the specific events mentioned in the superscription. Amos Hakham adopts the position of Rabbi Joshua, that all Psalms were composed for the public and do not relate directly to David's personal experiences. Therefore, he concludes that this verse is in fact a general prayer, applicable to all enemies of David and the Israelite nation.

Several other commentators maintain that even these ostensibly explicit references to other nations still refer to Saul and his men, following the superscription:

- Rashi (v. 6): "Bestir Yourself to bring all nations to account" – may You judge the wicked people *as You would the nations*. On them You should have no mercy (cf. his comments to v. 9).
- Ibn Ezra (v. 6): "Do not have mercy on traitors" – from whichever nation they derive [even if they are from Israel].
- Radak (v. 9): As You mock all the nations who deny You – annulling their [evil] thoughts and plots, so too may You mock these [i.e., Saul and his men].[5]

Rashi, Ibn Ezra, and Radak espouse the view that (1) David originally composed this Psalm as a personal prayer for salvation from Saul and his men; and (2) *All* references to enemies in this Psalm must allude to Saul and his men, even those where the plain sense of the text may have indicated otherwise.

The methodological considerations involved in an analysis of Psalms, even those with specific historical superscriptions, are difficult to resolve. Even if David composed psalms related to his personal life, the psalms are expanded to more general formulations so that everyone may use them as prayers. It appears most productive to treat the psalms with the historical superscriptions as a form of intertextual "midrash" on the book of Samuel, rather than a tool that will unlock *peshat* in the narratives of the book of Samuel.

THE PSALMS

Psalm 142

> A *maskil* of David, while he was in the cave. A prayer.... Look at my right and see – I have no friend, there is nowhere I can flee, no one cares about me.... Listen to my cry, for I have been brought very low; save me from my pursuers, for they are too strong for me. Free me from my prison, that I may praise Your Name. The righteous shall glory in me for Your gracious dealings with me.

Psalm 142 appears consistent with the image of David's purity portrayed in the narratives in Samuel. While hiding in a cave from Saul and his men (see 1 Samuel 22:1; 24:3), David felt isolated and frightened. Despite the threat to his life, however, he did not ask God to obliterate his enemies, nor did he even ridicule them. Instead, he asked only that God deliver him from danger so he could serve God in peace.

Reading this Psalm, one may imagine the anguish that plagued David as he fled from Saul. One also senses David's religious resolve as he asked to be spared so that God's Name would be sanctified among righteous people (v. 8).

Psalm 57

Psalm 142 stands alone in conveying this theme of David's purity. In Psalm 57, another prayer associated with David as he hid in a cave from Saul, the Psalm employs a different, more hostile, tone:

> For the leader; *al tashhet*. Of David. A *michtam*; when he fled from Saul into a cave. Have mercy on me, O God, have mercy on me, for I seek refuge in You.... He will reach down from heaven and deliver me: God will send down His steadfast love; my persecutor reviles. As for me, I lie down among man-eating

lions whose teeth are spears and arrows, whose tongue is a sharp sword. They prepared a net for my feet to ensnare me; they dug a pit for me, but they fell into it. My heart is firm, O God; my heart is firm; I will sing, I will chant a hymn.

This Psalm echoes the themes of Psalm 142, praying for salvation from enemies and remaining steadfastly focused on God and His reputation. Here, however, the psalmist also describes his pursuers in negative terms, poetically depicting their brutality and viciousness (vv. 4–5). Additionally, the psalmist appears gratified that his antagonists fall into the snare which they had set for him (v. 7).

Psalm 59
In Psalm 59, associated with the narrative when Saul sent men to surround David's house (see 1 Samuel 19), David appears even more resentful of his enemies:

> Save me from evildoers, deliver me from murderers. For see, they lie in wait for me; fierce men plot against me for no offense of mine, for no transgression, O Lord; for no guilt of mine do they rush to array themselves against me. Look, rouse Yourself on my behalf! They come each evening growling like dogs, roaming the city. They rave with their mouths…But You, O Lord, laugh at them…Do not kill them lest my people be unmindful; with Your power make wanderers of them; bring them low, O our Shield, the Lord.…Let them be trapped by their pride, and by the imprecations and lies they utter. Your fury put an end to them; put an end to them that they be no more; that it may be known to the ends of the earth that God does rule over Jacob. Selah.

This Psalm contains several elements we have seen in the others: prayer for salvation from enemies (verses 2–3, 10–11), and the request for the sanctification of God's Name (verse 14). However, the psalmist displays even more hostility towards his enemies, calling them dogs, the lowliest of all animals in Tanakh.[6] The psalmist petitions God to destroy his enemies slowly so that all people can witness their demise and realize that God is against them (see Rashi, Radak on 59:12). Applying this psalm to David's life, it conveys the sense that David harbored much resentment toward Saul and his men.

Psalm 63
Psalm 63, associated with David's hiding in the Wilderness of Judah, prays for the violent death of his enemies:

> God, You are my God; I search for You, my soul for You, my body yearns for You, as a parched and thirsty land that has no water.... May those who seek to destroy my life enter the depths of the earth. May he be gutted by the sword; may they be prey for jackals. But the king[7] shall rejoice in God; all who swear by Him shall exult, when the mouth of liars is stopped.

Applying the Psalms to the Saul-David narrative, Radak (on v. 11) explains that David first prayed for Saul (his singular foe) to be killed by the sword, and then for Saul's men to be prey for jackals. David harbored great anger toward Saul and his men, praying for their destruction, using harsh language against them and even promising to praise God at their downfall.

Psalm 18
Psalm 18 (found in variant form in II Samuel 22) is identified as a hymn of triumph over David's enemies: "To the chief musician, of David, the servant of the Lord, who spoke to the Lord the words of this song on the day that the Lord delivered him from the hand of all his enemies, and from the hand of Saul" (Psalm 18:1). The psalmist stresses the triumph of good over evil. The five Psalms we have considered identify a layer of deep resentment David felt toward Saul and his men throughout the pursuit. While maintaining allegiance to God and praying for his own personal salvation as well as the sanctification of God's Name, David also expressed deep bitterness towards his enemies and wished them dead. David also rejoiced at their downfall.

The above analysis uses the historical superscriptions to create a midrashic framework for imagining David's feelings toward Saul and his men. According to Amos Hakham, Psalms are written in generic formulas so that they may apply to different situations. One is not obligated to draw conclusions from possible allusions to Saul and his men, since they may refer to enemies in general. Regardless, these Psalms effectively serve as a "biblical Midrash" that offer additional dimensions of understanding to the narratives in Samuel.

THE TEXT OF SAMUEL

After analyzing the Psalms, we may revisit some of the passages in the book of Samuel pertaining to the relationship between David and Saul. In II Samuel 4, Saul's son Ish-bosheth was assassinated. As with the Amalekite youth in chapter one, David had the assassins put to death. Consistent with his position discussed earlier, Abarbanel maintains that David wanted to protect the institution of monarchy.

More significant, however, is David's justification of killing Ish-bosheth's assassins:

> The man who told me in Ziklag that Saul was dead thought he was bringing good news. But instead of rewarding him for the news, I seized him and killed him. How much more, then, when wicked people have killed a blameless man in bed in his own house! I will certainly avenge his blood on you, and I will rid the earth of you (II Samuel 4:10–11).

From this statement, we may infer that David believed that Saul was blameworthy and deserved his death, and that in contrast Ish-bosheth was unjustly killed. Although David's reasoning may be understood in other ways, this explanation is consistent with the mood conveyed in the Psalms we considered above. Perhaps David still harbored animosity toward Saul.

We find further evidence of David's continued resentment towards Saul when Michal (Saul's daughter and David's wife) became enraged after seeing David wildly dancing before the Ark. After Michal censured David for his un-kingly behavior, David snapped back at her, "It was before the Lord who chose me instead of your father and all his family and appointed me ruler over the Lord's people Israel!" (II Samuel 6:21).

Let us now return to David's stunning restraint from killing Saul:

> As the Lord lives, the Lord Himself will strike him down, or his time will come and he will die; or he will go down to battle and perish. But the Lord forbid that I should lay a hand on the Lord's anointed! (1 Samuel 26:10–11).

Although David stopped Abishai from assassinating Saul, he simultaneously prayed for the death of the monarch through natural or Divine causes. These verses, read in light of the Psalms, capture the powerful emotional conflict David felt at those moments.

The text appears to portray David's mixed feelings towards Saul in chapter 24, his first opportunity to kill the monarch:

> Please, sir, take a close look at the corner of your cloak my hand; for when I cut off the corner of your cloak, I did not kill you. You must see plainly that I have done nothing evil or rebellious, and I have never wronged you. Yet you are bent on taking my life.
>
> May the Lord judge between you and me! And may he take vengeance upon you for me, but my hand will never touch you....
>
> Against whom has the king of Israel come out? Whom are you pursuing? A dead dog? A single flea?
>
> May the Lord be arbiter and may He judge between you and me! May He take note and uphold my cause, and vindicate me against you!" (1 Samuel 24:12–16).

In his extended plea to Saul, David oscillates between a position of love and humility (please, sir ... against whom has the king of Israel come out), and one of hostility and vengeance (may the Lord judge ...). From our above analysis of the Psalms, it seems that David was caught between his profound love for his father-in-law and God's anointed, and his seething hostility towards his unjust and ruthless pursuer.

CONCLUSION

By using the Psalms ascribed to the period when David was pursued by Saul as an intertextual midrashic tool, one may conclude that David's feelings towards Saul were far more complex than a casual reading of the book of Samuel would suggest. Additionally, David never forgot Saul's conduct toward him. David's outburst at Michal and the subtler reference in the story of Ish-bosheth indicate that his bitterness was very much alive. These insights cast new light on the narratives in the book of Samuel as well.

We may now return to our original inquiry – why did David spare Saul? Once we have established that David did not have a purely forgiving attitude towards Saul, it would appear that the assertion of Ralbag and Abarbanel, that David was partially motivated by his own self-protection, has merit.

But perhaps the opposite may be argued. From the Psalms and from David's references to Saul in the book of Samuel, it is clear that David was constantly tormented by the king. David reacted as anyone would have – most likely with even greater intensity – with animosity, exasperation, and feelings of destructiveness. Yet, he was able to transcend his powerful emotions, and did not act on them. It is difficult to imagine that the mere desire to protect the institution of the monarchy would fully explain David's stifling of his burning desire to eliminate Saul. It is far more plausible that David's immense piety intervened at those critical moments and prompting him to exercise restraint: how could he kill God's anointed?[8]

In fact, some commentators explicate the superscription, *al tashhet* (see Psalm 57:1; 58:1; 59:1), in reference to the dual nature of David's prayer. Taking the phrase *al tashhet* to mean "do not destroy," some assert that David is praying for Saul not to destroy David (see Rashi on 57:1), but others explain that David is praying that he not destroy Saul (see Alsheikh on 57:1). Malbim agrees with Alsheikh's interpretation of *al tashhet*, deriving its meaning from David's command to Abishai (1 Samuel 26:9), *al tashhitehu* (do not do him violence). Rashi combines these two approaches in his commentary on 57:2, "'Have mercy on me, have mercy' – have mercy on me that I will not kill, and that I will not be killed."

This interpretation is consistent with *Midrash Psalms*, "Rabbi Isaac said, just as David prayed that he should not fall into the hands of Saul, so too he prayed that Saul should not fall into his hands" (7:13).

While the Psalms offer insight into David's feelings of hostility towards Saul, this conclusion serves only to highlight David's greatness and piety. David did not disregard life-threatening hostility directed at him. He was a real person with passionate human drives who at times wanted to lash out at his enemies, while other times was restrained by pragmatic and religious considerations. Our reading of the synthesized portrait of David from both Samuel and the Psalms shows a tormented, conflicted individual, one who passionately loved and resented his pursuer simultaneously.

In David's opportunities to kill Saul, he was just barely able to restrain himself and his men. In his piety, David recognized that Saul was God's chosen one. David's staggering self-control, in the heat of such potent emotions, truly places him as one of the most exemplary righteous people in our history.

NOTES

1. See also II Samuel 4:9–12, where David had Ish-bosheth's assassins executed, and Abarbanel *ad loc.*
2. For discussions of this balance, see e.g., Shalom Carmy, "To Get the Better of Words: An Apology for *Yir'at Shamayim* in Academic Jewish Studies," *Torah U-Madda Journal* 2 (1990), pp. 7–24; Howard Deitcher, "Between Angels and Mere Mortals: Nechama Leibowitz's Approach to the Study of Biblical Characters," *Journal of Jewish Education*, 66:1–2 (Spring/Summer 2000), pp. 8–22; Asher Friedman, "Imitate the Ramban, not the Professors – An Interview with Shalom Carmy," *Hamevaser*, 38:1 (2000); Yaakov Medan, *David u-Bat Sheva: ha-Het, ha-Onesh, ve-ha-Tikkun* (Hebrew) (Alon Shevut: Tevunot, 2002), pp. 7–24; Joel B. Wolowelsky, "*Kibbud Av* and *Kibbud Avot*: Moral Education and Patriarchal Critiques," *Tradition* 33:4 (Summer 1999), pp. 35–44; Joel B. Wolowelsky, "Abraham's Stories," in *Rav Shalom Banayikh: Essays Presented to Rabbi Shalom Carmy by Friends and Students in Celebration of Forty Years of Teaching*, ed. Hayyim Angel and Yitzchak Blau (Jersey City, NJ: Ktav, 2012), pp. 385–401.
3. One also might include Psalms 34 and 60, which David composed in Philistia while in flight from Saul.
4. See Amos Hakham (*Da'at Mikra: Psalms* [Hebrew] [Jerusalem: Mosad HaRav Kook, 1979], vol. 1), introduction pp. 15–18, for a fuller discussion of this topic.
5. On v. 6, Radak advances a novel interpretation: David is praying for the Day of Judgment in Messianic times. He observes that the entire verse does not fit into the general framework of the Psalm.
6. See, e.g., I Samuel 17:43; 24:14; II Samuel 3:8; 9:8; 16:9; Ecclesiastes 9:4.
7. Rashi and Radak explain that this refers to David, who was already anointed (and therefore viewed himself as a king already); cf. *Megillah* 14a–b.
8. The position of Ralbag and Abarbanel does seem in place, however, when David executed the Amalekite youth and Ish-bosheth's assassins.

Psalm 51:
David's Repentance from His Sin with Bathsheba and Uriah

One of the most beloved figures – arguably *the* most beloved – in Israel's history, is King David. He continues to inspire with his spectacular faith and kingship through his presence in the book of Psalms and the narratives in the books of Samuel and Chronicles. We pray for his descendant to herald the messianic era. The painful episode of Bathsheba and Uriah, involving grave sins pertaining to adultery and murder, is all the more wrenching coming from David. Traditional interpreters must offer a fair reading of the biblical text while maintaining proper reverence for our heroes.[1]

In his analysis of the passage, Abarbanel insists that David is guilty of adultery and murder. He cites the celebrated talmudic passage: "Whoever says that David sinned is merely erring" (*Shabbat* 56a). Although this line attempts to mitigate the extent of David's sins by stating that Uriah had given Bathsheba a *get* (writ of divorce), and Uriah was guilty of death as a rebel against the throne, Abarbanel rejects this understanding. The prophet Nathan explicitly accuses

---

This essay is adapted from my article, "The Yoke of Repentance: David's Post-Sin Conduct in the Book of Samuel and Psalm 51," at yutorah.org.

David of sinning, and David confesses and repents (II Samuel chapter 12). In fact, Rav, the leading disciple of Rabbi Yehudah ha-Nasi (known simply as "Rabbi"), dismisses his teacher's defense of David on the spot: "Rabbi, who is descended from David, seeks to defend him and expounds [the verse] in David's favor." Therefore, concludes Abarbanel,

> These words of our Sages are the ways of *derash*, and I have no need to respond to them.... I prefer to say that [David] sinned greatly and confessed greatly and repented fully and accepted his punishment, and in this manner, he attained atonement for his sins.[2]

Although Abarbanel presents himself as an independent interpreter in this instance, he has ample precedent within rabbinic tradition. A number of talmudic sources do not mitigate David's sins. For example, there are opinions that Bathsheba was possibly a married woman or certainly a married woman[3]; that the initial encounter should be viewed halakhically as the rape of a married woman since Bathsheba was not in a position to decline[4]; that David was culpable for the death of Uriah[5]; and that Joab bears guilt for failing to defy David's immoral orders regarding Uriah.[6] The unambiguous textual evidence against David seems to have convinced Abarbanel that it was unnecessary to cite additional sources beyond Rav's dismissal of his teacher's defense of David.[7]

The *peshat* reading of David's sins yields several significant lessons. Rabbi Yehudah he-Hasid observes that this story warns of the immense power of lust (*Sefer Hasidim* 619). More broadly, Rabbi Amnon Bazak observes that this story exemplifies the absolute honesty and integrity of Tanakh. Prophecy shows no favoritism and judges all people – even the beloved David – by the standards of the Torah.[8]

Abarbanel highlights the religious inspiration deriving from David's repentance. Similarly, the Talmud views this narrative as the supreme model for individual repentance:

> Rabbi Yohanan said in the name of Rabbi Shimon b. Yohai: David was not the kind of man to do that act [Bathsheba in-

cident], nor was Israel the kind of people to do that act [the Golden Calf incident].... Why, then, did they act thus? In order to teach that if an individual has sinned [and hesitates about the effect of repentance] he could be referred to the individual [David], and if a community commits a sin they should be told: Go to the community [to appreciate the effect of repentance] (*Avodah Zarah* 4b–5a).

In this essay, we will follow the lead of this Gemara and Abarbanel, and explore aspects of David's exemplary process of repentance in the narratives in the book of Samuel and in Psalm 51.

DAVID'S ACCEPTANCE OF SIN AND RETRIBUTION

Though God rejected King Saul and his dynasty for Saul's sins, God allowed David and his dynasty to remain on the throne for centuries despite David's sins. Rabbi Yosef Albo (*Ikkarim* 4:26) and Abarbanel suggest that since David's sins were in the realm of human frailty, and not in his role as king, the monarchy could endure. In contrast, Saul sinned specifically in his role as king, and therefore forfeited his throne.

Rabbi Yaakov Medan challenges this answer. David abused his royal authority by sending his servants to take a hero's wife, and then had Uriah killed by using the army and issuing orders to Joab. These sins emanated specifically from David in his capacity as king. Rabbi Medan therefore suggests that God allowed David to remain on the throne – despite his misuse of power – because David immediately confessed and repented: "David said to Nathan, 'I stand guilty before the Lord!'" (II Samuel 12:13). In contrast, Saul first attempted to deflect his guilt, and only after the piercing prophecy of Samuel did he finally admit his wrongdoing.[9] Regardless of whether Rabbi Medan is "correct" regarding God's rationale of retaining David on the throne, there certainly is evidence of David's repentance in the ensuing narratives in the book of Samuel.

A hallmark feature of biblical narrative is "dual causality." God often reveals His plans through prophecy, and then characters act on their own free will and unwittingly fulfill the divine plan.[10] Following the Bathsheba episode, Nathan prophesies to David that he will be punished from within his household:

> "... Therefore the sword shall never depart from your House – because you spurned Me by taking the wife of Uriah the Hittite and making her your wife." Thus said the Lord: "I will make a calamity rise against you from within your own house; I will take your wives and give them to another man before your very eyes and he shall sleep with your wives under this very sun. You acted in secret, but I will make this happen in the sight of all Israel and in broad daylight" (II Samuel 12:10–12).

The death of David's infant son (chapter 12), Amnon's rape of Tamar and being killed by Absalom (chapter 13), and Absalom's rebellion, rape of David's concubines, and being killed by Joab (chapters 15–18) are thereby cast as divine retribution for David's sins. Amnon and Absalom sinned out of their own free will, and not out of a desire to fulfill Nathan's prophecy. Unlike all the other characters in the narrative, David was aware of the divine plan of retribution, since Nathan had prophesied it to him. David did not know specifically how this punishment would unfold, yet his consciousness of his sin and the divine decree decisively affected his behavior.

Jonathan Jacobs suggests that the narrative depicting David's contrition while the child was still alive, and then calming down after the son's death, is intended as a contrast with the perception of David's officers. The officers mistakenly assumed that David was acting as a normal father with a gravely ill child, and therefore expected David to be inconsolable after learning of the child's death. However, David was conscious that his son's illness was a divine decree for his sin, and therefore was crying to atone for his sins. Once the child died, David sensed atonement and was relieved, and went to the House of God before eating.[11]

This contrast of perceptions between David and the other characters continues into the narratives about Amnon and Absalom. After Amnon raped Tamar, David learned of this horrific act and was outraged (II Samuel 13:21). Shockingly, however, he did not punish Amnon. Moreover, Absalom began his rebellion by telling people that he – unlike his father David – would judge people fairly (II Samuel 15:3–4). Although Absalom was a demagogue, his claim was fundamentally correct, since David did not punish Amnon for an egregious sin (Abarbanel, Yehudah Kiel[12]).

Why, however, did David refrain from punishing Amnon? Likely following the prophetic criticism of David's spoiling Adonijah later on (I Kings 1:6), the Septuagint and Josephus suggest that David exhibited favoritism toward his son Amnon. However, Yehudah Elitzur cogently maintains that unlike the other characters who acted on their own, David understood that Amnon's rape of Tamar was in part retribution for David's own sins. This knowledge paralyzed him from meting out justice when his son committed a similar crime.[13]

During Absalom's rebellion, David surprised his priests Zadok and Abiathar by ordering them to keep the Ark in Jerusalem:

> "Take the Ark of God back to the city. If I find favor with the Lord, He will bring me back and let me see it and its abode. And if He should say, 'I do not want you,' I am ready; let Him do with me as He pleases" (II Samuel 15:25–26).

David similarly considered Shimei's curses and insults to be possible divine retribution, and therefore did not allow Abishai to harm Shimei:

> But the king said, "What has this to do with you, you sons of Zeruiah? He is abusing [me] only because the Lord told him to abuse David; and who is to say, 'Why did You do that?'" (16:10; cf. 19:24).

Most strikingly, David ordered his army not to harm Absalom (18:5). Joab disobeyed by killing Absalom (18:10–15), and then sharply rebuked David for betraying his loyal followers by mourning for the enemy (19:6–8). Yehudah Elitzur again maintains that David does not appear to be acting merely out of parental favoritism. Unlike all the other characters, David understood that Absalom's rebellion was also divine retribution for his own sin of Bathsheba and Uriah. The weight of his sin and his acceptance of the divine decree crippled him. Throughout the narrative, then, David acknowledged that all was from God, and that he was in God's hands. He accepted divine retribution, and the weight of his sins stymied him in his conduct with Amnon and Absalom.[14] Elitzur argues further that David's brokenhearted contrition is all the more meaningful, since David had such a strong personality. These features make David the ultimate role model of repentance.[15]

PSALM 51

Beyond David's contrition expressed in the book of Samuel, Psalm 51 contributes additional dimensions to this discussion:

> For the leader. A psalm of David, when Nathan the prophet came to him after he had come to Bathsheba (Psalm 51:1–2).

Psalm 51 depicts David's feelings of remorse and repentance, as he attempted to rebuild his relationship with God after his sin. Ibn Ezra and Radak maintain that David composed this psalm after Nathan left the palace following his rebuke of David in II Samuel chapter 12. Alternatively, Amos Hakham suggests that David may have composed the psalm while Nathan was still in the palace. Either way, the psalm functions as an intertextual "midrashic" extension of David's poignant confession, "I stand guilty before the Lord" (II Samuel 12:13).[16]

The penitent psalmist pleads for forgiveness, and expresses an overwhelming sense of his sin: "Indeed I was born with iniquity; with sin my mother conceived me" (Psalm 51:7). Several commentators, including Rashi, Ibn Ezra, and Malbim, explain the verse as a plea for mercy and an attempt to mitigate the sin, because lust is part of human nature. Meiri, however, maintains that the psalmist is poetically exaggerating his sin, proclaiming that he feels as though he has been sinning since the womb (see also Amos Hakham). It is unlikely, according to Meiri, that the psalmist is attempting to mitigate his sin. Rather, quite the opposite – he is consumed by his guilt, and pours his broken heart out to God.

After pleading to God to restore their relationship, the psalmist prays, "I will teach transgressors Your ways, that sinners may return to You" (Psalm 51:15). If God accepts his repentance, others who have sinned will be inspired and find their way back to God, as well.

The psalm concludes with a national prayer:

> May it please You to make Zion prosper; rebuild the walls of Jerusalem. Then You will want sacrifices offered in righteousness, burnt and whole offerings; then bulls will be offered on Your altar (Psalm 51:20–21).

The plea for the building of Jerusalem's walls seems to refer to the period after the destruction of the First Temple, since Jerusalem's walls were intact from before David's lifetime until the Babylonians breached them prior to the destruction of the Temple. Drawing from a midrashic reading (*Leviticus Rabbah* 7:2), Rashi suggests that after praying for personal atonement, David prayed for the Temple to be built by Solomon. However, the verse only mentions the walls of Jerusalem, not the Temple. Moreover, people could offer sacrifices on other shrines (*bamot*) during David's lifetime, whereas the final two verses of this psalm suggest that the people could not bring offerings without the Temple.

Ibn Ezra quotes a Spanish rabbi who therefore explained that a later writer added these two verses after the destruction of the First Temple. This writer drew inspiration from David's prayer for forgiveness and pleaded to God: please forgive us as a nation as You forgave David as an individual. In this reading, the text of the psalm itself epitomizes the idea that David serves as a model of repentance for later generations.[17]

It is fitting that we open every Amidah with a verse from Psalm 51: "O Lord, open my lips, and let my mouth declare Your praise" (verse 17). Although it is the supreme privilege to be invited to stand before God, we begin with a humble expression of our unworthiness to pray. This introductory verse becomes all the more poignant when we know its context in Psalm 51, experiencing David's contrition as he struggled to restore his relationship with God. David's repentance from his sin of Bathsheba and Uriah, both in the Samuel narratives and in Psalm 51, has inspired all later generations, setting the tone for contrition and rebuilding a relationship with God:

> Rabbi Shemuel b. Nahmani citing Rabbi Yonathan explained: The saying of David the son of Yishai and the saying of the man raised on high (II Samuel 23:1), [means, it is] the saying of David the son of Jesse who established firmly the yoke [discipline] of repentance (*Mo'ed Katan* 16b).

NOTES

1. For discussions of this balance, see e.g., Amnon Bazak, *Ad ha-Yom ha-Zeh: Until This Day: Fundamental Questions in Bible Teaching* (Hebrew), ed. Yoshi Farajun (Tel Aviv: Yediot Aharonot, 2013), pp. 432–470; Shalom Carmy, "To Get the Better of Words: An Apology for *Yir'at Shamayim* in Academic Jewish Studies," *Torah U-Madda Journal* 2 (1990), pp. 7–24; Rabbi Aharon Lichtenstein, "A Living Torah" (Hebrew), in *Hi Sihati: Al Derekh Limmud ha-Tanakh*, ed. Yehoshua Reiss (Jerusalem: Maggid, 2013), pp. 17–30; Yaakov Medan, *David u-Bathsheba: ha-Het, ha-Onesh, ve-ha-Tikkun* (Hebrew) (Alon Shevut: Tevunot, 2002), pp. 7–24; Joel B. Wolowelsky, "*Kibbud Av* and *Kibbud Avot*: Moral Education and Patriarchal Critiques," *Tradition* 33:4 (Summer 1999), pp. 35–44.
2. Commentary on Samuel (Jerusalem: Torah ve-Da'at, 1955), pp. 342–343.
3. *Bava Metzia* 59a; *Sanhedrin* 107a; *Midrash Psalms* 3:4.
4. *Ketuvot* 9a.
5. *Yoma* 22b; *Kiddushin* 43a.
6. *Sanhedrin* 49a.
7. Abarbanel was not the first medieval interpreter to assert David's guilt, either. Rabbi Yehudah b. Nathan (Rashi's son-in-law, in *Teshuvot Hakhmei Provencia*, vol. 1 no. 71), Rabbi Yeshayah of Trani (on Psalm 51:1; but see his remarks on II Samuel 12:4, where he adopts the view that Uriah had given Bathsheba a *get*), and Rabbi Yosef ibn Caspi (on II Samuel 11:6) preceded him in understanding that Bathsheba was a married woman. Ralbag (*To'elet* 8) preceded Abarbanel by insisting that Uriah cannot be judged as a rebel against the throne and therefore his death was unjustified.
8. Amnon Bazak, *Ad ha-Yom ha-Zeh*, p. 469. Scholars have observed that there is no known analogy to this honest, critical stance toward one's own heroes in ancient Near Eastern literature. See, for example, George Mendenhall, *Ancient Israel's Faith and History: An Introduction to the Bible in Context* (Louisville, KY: Westminster John Knox Press, 2001), p. 112.
9. Yaakov Medan, *David u-Bathsheba*, p. 38; cf. Rabbi Joseph B. Soloveitchik, *Fate and Destiny: From the Holocaust to the State of Israel* (*Kol Dodi Dofek*) (Hoboken, NJ: Ktav, 2000), pp. 21–22; Yehudah Elitzur, "The War Against Amalek: Saul's War Against Amalek and Its Place in Prophetic Thought" (Hebrew), in Elitzur, *Yisrael ve-ha-Mikra: Mehkarim Geografi'im Histori'im ve-Hagoti'im* (Hebrew), ed. Yoel Elitzur and Amos Frisch (Ramat Gan: Bar Ilan University Press, 1999), pp. 113–120.
10. For further discussion of dual causality in the David narratives, see Hayyim Angel, "Dual Causality and Characters' Knowledge: The Interaction between the Human and the Divine," in Angel, *The Keys to the Palace: Essays Exploring the Religious Value of Reading the Bible* (New York: Kodesh Press, 2017), pp. 168–182.

11. Jonathan Jacobs, "The Death of the Child of David from Bathsheba (II Samuel 12:13–25)" (Hebrew), *Megadim* 50 (2009), pp. 135–142.
12. Yehudah Kiel, *Da'at Mikra: II Samuel* (Hebrew) (Jerusalem: Mosad HaRav Kook, 1981), p. 447. Prior to his sin, David was praised specifically for his just reign: "David reigned over all Israel, and David executed true justice among all his people" (II Samuel 8:15).
13. Elitzur, "David Son of Jesse – A Model for Penitents" (Hebrew), in *Yisrael ve-ha-Mikra*, pp. 144–149. Cf. Yehudah Kiel, *Da'at Mikra: II Samuel*, p. 435.
14. See also Ari Mermelstein, "Retribution, Repentance, Restoration: The Motives and Message Underlying Absalom's Rebellion," *Nahalah* 1 (1999), pp. 51–64.
15. Elitzur, "David Son of Jesse – A Model for Penitents," p. 148.
16. Amos Hakham, *Da'at Mikra: Psalms* vol. 1 (Hebrew) (Jerusalem: Mosad Harav Kook, 1979), p. 296.
17. For an overview of traditional views on the authorship of the different Psalms, see the introductory chapter in this volume.

God Insists on Truth:
Rabbinic Evaluations of Two Audacious Biblical Prayers

In this article, we consider the diversity of response to two sharply formulated prayers in Tanakh. Habakkuk appears to accuse God of poor judgment by allowing the wicked Babylonians to conquer Judah, and then boldly demands a response. Psalm 89 lashes out at God for abrogating the permanent covenant He had struck with the Davidic dynasty.

Traditional interpreters assume that everything in Tanakh is divinely inspired and is applicable to all later generations (see *Megillah* 14a). At the same time, several Midrashim and later exegetes are uncomfortable with the bluntness of these prayers, and therefore attempt to restrict their applicability. These commentators adopt variations of at least five options:

1. The prophet/psalmist acted religiously appropriately, and therefore we should emulate his prayer.
2. The prophet/psalmist acted religiously appropriately, but most people have not attained a sufficiently high spiritual level to

---

This essay is adapted from my article in *Creating Space between Peshat and Derash: A Collection of Studies on Tanakh* (Jersey City, NJ: Ktav-Sephardic Publication Foundation, 2011), pp. 154-162.

emulate that kind of prayer. Therefore they should speak more diffidently before God.
3. The prophet/psalmist was objectively wrong himself.
4. The prophet/psalmist was quoting someone else rather than speaking for himself.
5. The text needs to be supplemented or reinterpreted in order to remove the sting of the more literal reading.

HABAKKUK

How long, O Lord, shall I cry out and You not listen, shall I shout to You, "Violence!" And You not save? Why do You make me see iniquity [why] do You look upon wrong? – Raiding and violence are before me, strife continues and contention goes on. That is why decision fails and justice never emerges; for the villain hedges in the just man – therefore judgment emerges deformed (Habakkuk 1:2–4).

I will stand on my watch, take up my station at the post, and wait to see what He will say to me, what He will reply to my complaint (2:1).[1]

Habakkuk had difficulty with the favor God was to show the Babylonians at the time of the destruction of the Temple. Although Israel may have deserved punishment for its sins, this punishment should not have come at the hands of a nation far more wicked (Abarbanel on 1:13). Habakkuk maintained that the success of the wicked Babylonians would reduce faithfulness, since people would conclude that there is no justice in the world (Ibn Ezra, Radak on 1:4). Additionally, Habakkuk expresses frustration that God had not yet responded to his prayers, suggesting a long history of protest prior to the opening of the biblical book.

One Midrash is uncomfortable with Habakkuk's tone and sharply criticizes him:

"Keep your mouth from being rash" (Ecclesiastes 5:1).... When Habakkuk said, "I will stand on my watch, take up my station at the post" (Habakkuk 2:1).... This teaches that he drew a form, and stood in its midst. He said, "I will not move from here until You answer me."... God replied, "You are not an ignoramus, but rather a Torah scholar!"... When Habakkuk heard this, he fell on his face and supplicated. He said, "Master of the Universe! Do not judge me as a willful transgressor, but rather as an inadvertent sinner [*shogeg*]." This is what is written, "A prayer of the prophet Habakkuk. In the mode of *Shigionoth*" (Habakkuk 3:1) (*Midrash Psalms* 7:17; cf. 90:7).

This Midrash deems Habakkuk guilty of speaking rashly before God, emulating an ignoramus rather than a prophet. It proceeds to explain Habakkuk 3 – prefaced with *al shigionoth* (midrashically explained as deriving from *sh-g-g*, "error") – as a psalm of repentance by the prophet.[2]

A different approach is espoused in the Talmud, where Habakkuk's story is likened to that of Honi the Circle Drawer: "[Honi] thereupon drew a circle and stood within it in the same way as the prophet Habakkuk had done." Both brazenly and successfully demanded responses from God. Habakkuk received a divine response,[3] and Honi got the rain he had demanded. In the Talmud, both figures are praised for their saintliness and for God's positive responses. Despite Honi's success, however, Shimon ben Shetah was deeply concerned with his conduct:

> If you were not Honi, I would have excommunicated you.... But what can I do to you who acts petulantly before the Omnipresent and He grants your desire, as a son who acts petulantly before his father and he grants his desires (*Ta'anit* 23a).

Shimon ben Shetah insisted that it was religiously inappropriate to make such demands of God.[4] Nevertheless, he begrudgingly recognized that Honi enjoyed a privileged relationship with God.[5] This talmudic passage appears to espouse the view that Habakkuk and Honi were objectively correct in their prayers. Concerned that others might emulate them, Shimon ben Shetah restricted the applicability of these prayers to an exclusive elite.[6]

Ibn Ezra (on Habakkuk 1:1, 12) adopts a different approach to Habakkuk's prayers. Rather than admit that a prophet spoke for himself, Ibn Ezra asserts that Habakkuk was quoting others of his generation. Thus Ibn Ezra avoids the need to ask whether this prophetic prayer may be used as a model or not, since Habakkuk was not the originator of those words.

Then again, perhaps Habakkuk was concerned about the religious ramifications the destruction likely would cause. Most commentators do not ascribe these words to other speakers, nor do they think Habakkuk was repenting in chapter 3. God responded to Habakkuk without any tone of criticism. Therefore Habakkuk's prayer may have been fully appropriate, and God's positive response supports this view.[7]

PSALM 89

Psalm 89 is one of the most jarring of the psalms. For 38 verses, the psalmist speaks elatedly of God's eternal covenant with the Davidic monarchy. The psalm refers to Nathan's prophecy of an eternal dynasty to David:

> When your days are done and you lie with your fathers, I will raise up your offspring after you, one of your own issue, and I will establish his kingship. He shall build a house for My name, and I will establish his royal throne forever. I will be a father to him, and he shall be a son to Me. When he does wrong, I will chastise him with the rod of men and the affliction of mortals; but I will never withdraw My favor from him as I withdrew it from Saul, whom I removed to make room for you. Your house and your kingship shall ever be secure before you; your throne shall be established forever (II Samuel 7:12–16).

Picking up on that prophecy, the psalmist notes that God swore that the Davidic monarchy would endure forever, like the sun, moon, and heavens:

> I have made a covenant with My chosen one; I have sworn to My servant David: I will establish your offspring forever, I will

confirm your throne for all generations. Selah... I have found David, My servant; anointed him with My sacred oil. My hand shall be constantly with him, and My arm shall strengthen him. No enemy shall oppress him, no vile man afflict him... I will establish his line forever, his throne, as long as the heavens last... I will not violate My covenant, or change what I have uttered. I have sworn by My holiness, once and for all; I will not be false to David. His line shall continue forever, his throne, as the sun before Me, as the moon, established forever, an enduring witness in the sky. Selah (Psalm 89:4–38).

The psalm then turns abruptly in verses 39–52, as the psalmist explodes at the abrogation of the covenant when the monarchy ended. It reflects the cessation of the Davidic monarchy after the destruction of the First Temple in 586 BCE, when Zedekiah was the last king:

Yet You have rejected, spurned, and become enraged at Your anointed. You have repudiated the covenant with Your servant; You have dragged his dignity in the dust. You have breached all his defenses, shattered his strongholds (Psalm 89:39–41).

It appears that the psalmist is directly accusing God of violating His oath.[8]

Rashi mitigates the protest by inserting an admission of sin: "You have been meticulous with [David's] descendants to weigh their sins until You rejected and spurned them in the time of Zedekiah." From this point of view, the psalmist is shifting blame onto Israel, rather than accusing God. However, the flow of the psalm appears to militate against this reading. As Nathan had prophesied, sin would elicit punishment, but the monarchy itself was to endure forever:

I will establish his line forever, his throne, as long as the heavens last. If his sons forsake My Teaching and do not live by My rules; if they violate My laws, and do not observe My commands, I will punish their transgression with the rod, their iniquity with plagues. But I will not take away My steadfast love from him; I will not betray My faithfulness (Psalm 89:30–34; cf. II Samuel 7:12–16).

Nevertheless, one can appreciate why Rashi reinterpreted the verses. The plain sense of the text is sharp indeed.

Those who accept the simplest reading of the text must confront this challenge directly. Ibn Ezra (on 89:2) mentions a Spanish sage who considered this psalm blasphemous and therefore censored it: "In Spain, there was a great and pious sage, and this psalm was difficult for him. He would not read it, nor was he able to listen to it since the psalmist speaks sharply against God...." Ibn Ezra agrees that those verses are blasphemous, but he is unwilling to entertain the possibility that an inspired biblical psalmist would speak inappropriately. Therefore he asserts that the psalmist is quoting the words of the enemies of God who commit blasphemy.

Radak, in turn, censures the anonymous sage and Ibn Ezra:

> Many have expressed astonishment over how this psalmist could speak these words against God.... I am astonished by their astonishment, for the psalms were written through divine inspiration, and it is unthinkable that something in them is untrue! (Radak on 89:39).

Rabbi Yeshayah of Trani and Amos Hakham likewise consider these words to be of the psalmist. The words are by definition religiously acceptable, since they appear in the mouth of a divinely inspired writer. Providing a framework for these harsh words, Hakham quotes talmudic passages stating that the righteous do not flatter God. Rather, they stand honestly before their Creator, pouring out all their emotions.[9] Does this mean that everyone may emulate this style of prayer? That is a matter of debate, as was discussed in the case of Habakkuk (and Honi). In practice, Jewish liturgy generally did not include this psalm.[10]

GOD INSISTS ON TRUTH

Always sensitive to minor nuances, the Talmud compares the formulations of four verses scattered throughout Tanakh:

> For the Lord your God is God supreme and Lord supreme, the *great*, the *mighty*, and the *awesome* God (Deuteronomy 10:17).

O *great* and *mighty* God whose name is Lord of Hosts (Jeremiah 32:18).

O Lord, *great* and *awesome* God, who stays faithful to His covenant with those who love Him and keep His commandments! (Daniel 9:4).

And now, our God, *great, mighty*, and *awesome* God, who stays faithful to His covenant (Nehemiah 9:32).

Focusing on the fact that Moses had said "the great, the mighty, and the awesome God," the Sages recognized that Jeremiah and Daniel used only parts of that formulation and that the leaders of the prayer in Nehemiah 9 restored Moses' complete formula. They posited the following reasoning behind this development:

> Why were they called Men of the Great Assembly? Because they restored the crown of Divine attributes to its ancient completeness. Moses had said, "the great, the mighty, and the awesome God." Then Jeremiah came and said, "Foreigners are destroying His Temple! Where are His awesome deeds?" Therefore he omitted "awesome." Daniel came and said, "Foreigners are enslaving His sons. Where are His mighty deeds?" Therefore he omitted "mighty." But they came and said, "On the contrary! He performs mighty deeds by suppressing His wrath.... He performs awesome deeds, since were it not for the fear of Him, how could one nation persist among the nations!" But how could [Jeremiah and Daniel] abolish something established by Moses? Rabbi Eleazar said: Since they know that the Holy One, blessed be He, insists on truth, they would not ascribe false [things] to Him (*Yoma* 69b).

This talmudic passage sensitively balances the tension of truthfulness and deferential respect before God. On the one hand, the Sages praise the Men of the Great Assembly for their optimism and for restoring Moses' account of God's attributes to its original full form. Indeed, the Talmud gives them the final word, and the first benediction of the Amidah contains this complete formulation. At the same time, however, the Talmud applauds the profound religious integrity of Jeremiah and Daniel.

Throughout biblical tradition, the lions of faith have challenged God – already beginning with Abraham and Moses:

> Far be it from You to do such a thing, to bring death upon the innocent as well as the guilty, so that innocent and guilty fare alike. Far be it from You! Shall not the Judge of all the earth deal justly? (Genesis 18:25).

> Now, if You will forgive their sin [well and good]; but if not, erase me from the record which You have written! (Exodus 32:32).

One talmudic passage captures the daring spirit of Moses' prayer:

> Rabbi Abbahu said: Were it not explicitly written, it would be impossible to say such a thing: this teaches that Moses took hold of the Holy One, blessed be He, like a man who seizes his fellow by his garment and said before Him: Sovereign of the Universe, I will not let You go until You forgive and pardon them (*Berakhot* 32a).

Whether to pray for the manifestation of God's justice, or to intervene on Israel's behalf, prophets and other biblical writers often spoke brazenly before God. Precisely our spiritual heroes – who generally must be emulated – are those who enjoyed the most intimate relationships with God, affording them a certain comfort level that may be too great for most people. The diversity of rabbinic responses to these and related prayers attests to the power of this paradox that likely will never be resolved.

NOTES

1. The Hebrew reads *u-mah ashiv*, "what *I* will respond," to my complaint. Several commentators explain that other people wanted answers to the same questions the prophet had posed to God. Habakkuk therefore demands answers for himself and for the people who were rebuking him (Rashi, Kara, Ibn Ezra, Radak). Alternatively, Menahem Boleh (*Da'at Mikra: Habakkuk*, in *Twelve Prophets*, vol. 2 [Hebrew] [Jerusalem: Mosad ha-Rav Kook, 1990], p. 10), and the NJPS translation quoted above suggest that the verse should be understood as though it is read *u-mah yashiv*, "what He [God] would respond" to my complaint. It was modified either by Habakkuk or a later scribe as a euphemism like other *tikkunei soferim*. See also Shemuel Ahituv, *Mikra le-Yisrael: Habakkuk* (Tel Aviv: Am Oved, 2006), p. 39; Francis I. Andersen, *Habakkuk*: Anchor Bible (New York: Doubleday, 2001), p. 194. On *tikkunei soferim*, see, for example, Saul Lieberman, *Hellenism in Jewish Palestine* (New York: Jewish Theological Seminary, 1950), pp. 28–37; Moshe A. Zipor, "Some Notes on the Origin of the Tradition of the Eighteen *Tiqqune Soperim*," *Vetus Testamentum* 44 (1994), pp. 77–102.
2. Rashi and Kara (on 3:1) adopt this midrashic reading. Abarbanel (on 2:4) also criticizes Habakkuk for speaking too sharply. For a survey of views that are critical of Habakkuk's prayer, see Aron Pinker, "Was Habakkuk Presumptuous?" *Jewish Bible Quarterly* 32 (2004), pp. 27–34. As we will see below, there are indeed those who criticize Habakkuk for his prayer, but there are other means of responding as well.
3. For analysis of this response, see Hayyim Angel, "'The Righteous Shall Live By His Faith': Habakkuk and the Problem of Unfairness in the World," in Angel, *Peshat Isn't So Simple: Essays on Developing a Religious Methodology to Bible Study* (New York: Kodesh Press, 2014), pp. 286–298.
4. Cf. *Berakhot* 19a, where Rabbi Eleazar cites the Honi episode as an example of a person deserving excommuication for excessive brazenness toward God.
5. Two pages later in the Talmud, there is further criticism of speaking brazenly before God: "Levi ordained a fast but no rain fell. He thereupon exclaimed: Master of the Universe, You went up and took Your seat on high and have no mercy upon Your children. Rain fell but he became lame. Rabbi Eleazar said: Let a man never address himself in a reproachful manner towards God, seeing that one great man did so and he became lame, namely, Levi" (*Ta'anit* 25a).
6. Cf. Moshe Greenberg's assessment: "These heroes of faith have achieved a standing with God that ordinary mortals do not enjoy.... The situation of the ordinary mortal is quite different. With neither a vocation to God's service nor the heroism of these figures of legend, self-assertiveness and

autonomy in relation to God would be considered presumptuous...the storming of heaven by prophets hardly served as a model for the ordinary (or even the extraordinary) pious Israelite" ("On the Refinement of the Conception of Prayer in Hebrew Scriptures," *Association for Jewish Studies Review* 1 [1976], p. 58).

7. Francis I. Andersen (*Habakkuk*: Anchor Bible, p. 133) observes that there are no instances in Tanakh where God rebuked someone for questioning God's justice. In the book of Job, God criticized Job's shortsightedness but vindicated his justness as well. It is worth noting that one psalmist does rebuke those who question God's ways (Psalm 94:8–10), and that type of rebuke is unique in Psalms.

8. For a fuller discussion of the biblical approaches to the eternality of the Davidic covenant, see Hayyim Angel, "The Eternal Davidic Covenant in II Samuel Chapter 7 and Its Later Manifestations in the Bible," in *The Keys to the Palace: Essays Exploring the Religious Value of Reading the Bible* (New York: Kodesh Press, 2017), pp. 211–223.

9. Amos Hakham, *Da'at Mikra: Psalms* vol. 2 (Hebrew), (Jerusalem: Mosad ha-Rav Kook, 1979) pp. 156–157. See, for example, JT *Berakhot* 7:4 (11c); BT *Yoma* 69b.

10. Joseph Heinemann argues more generally that the Sages were unwilling to include protests against God in the fixed liturgy but were willing to protest against God in private prayers (*Prayer in the Talmud: Forms and Patterns* [Berlin: de Gruyter, 1977], pp. 193–207).

Psalms 90–107:
Rebuilding Faith After Crisis

We cannot know how the book of Psalms was composed. The following is a speculative midrashic-style effort at creating a coherent approach toward the organization of the five books of Psalms by the book's editors.[1]

Psalm 1 opens the book of Psalms by affirming God's justice and fairness in the world. Psalms 2 and 72 then form the bookends of another important theme in books 1–2 of Psalms: God's covenant with David and the Davidic dynasty:

> Why do nations assemble, and peoples plot vain things; kings of the earth take their stand, and regents intrigue together against the Lord and against His anointed?... [God responds:] "But I have installed My king on Zion, My holy mountain!" Let me tell of the decree: The Lord said to me, you are My son, I have fathered you this day (Psalm 2:1–2, 6–7).

> Of Solomon. O God, endow the king with Your judgments, the king's son with Your righteousness; that he may judge Your people rightly, Your lowly ones, justly... May his name be eternal; while the sun lasts, may his name endure; let men

---

This essay is adapted from my article, "The 'Story' Behind Psalms," in Angel, *Vision from the Prophet and Counsel from the Elders: A Survey of Nevi'im and Ketuvim* (New York: OU Press, 2013), pp. 235-240.

invoke his blessedness upon themselves; let all nations count him happy (Psalm 72:1–2, 17).

Thus, the bookends of books 1–2 teach that God is fair and that God has chosen the Davidic dynasty.

Book 3 opens with Psalm 73, which challenges God's fairness. The psalmist almost lost his faith as a result of the apparent injustice in this world:

> As for me, my feet had almost strayed, my steps were nearly led off course, for I envied the wanton; I saw the wicked at ease (Psalm 73:2–3).

Although the psalmist reaches resolution by the conclusion of the psalm, it is more complex than the straightforward faith in God's justice of Psalm 1.

Book 3 contains several psalms that speak about the destruction of the First Temple, and it climaxes with Psalm 89. After praising God for making an eternal covenant with the Davidic dynasty in the first 38 verses, the psalmist accuses God of abrogating that covenant at the time of the destruction when the monarchy ceased to exist:

> Yet You have rejected, spurned, and become enraged at Your anointed. You have repudiated the covenant with Your servant; You have dragged his dignity in the dust. You have breached all his defenses, shattered his strongholds… (Psalm 89:39–41).

The bookends of book 3 (Psalms 73, 89) thereby threaten the premises established in the bookends of books 1–2 (Psalms 1, 2, 72). Psalm 73 challenges God's fairness, and God's support for the Davidic dynasty likewise is in jeopardy in 89. At this point in the book of Psalms, the foundations upon which the book had rested are called into question. One cannot even appeal to David to pray, since his dynasty has stopped which itself is a central aspect of this crisis.

Only one person is capable of reversing this distressing trend. Book 4 opens with the one psalm ascribed to Moses,[2] famed for his brazen prayers before God:

> A prayer of Moses, the man of God… Turn, O Lord! How long? Show mercy to Your servants. Satisfy us at daybreak with Your steadfast love that we may sing for joy all our days. Give us joy for as long as You have afflicted us, for the years we have suffered misfortune. Let Your deeds be seen by Your servants, Your glory by their children. May the favor of the Lord, our God, be upon us; let the work of our hands prosper, O prosper the work of our hands! (Psalm 90:1, 13–17).

The psalmist employs language that Moses used during the episode of the Golden Calf (see Exodus 32:12): "Turn, O Lord! How long?" Just like after the Golden Calf when God wanted to sever His relationship with Israel, but Moses tenaciously refused to allow God to do so; so too in our exile, we insist that God not abandon us. Through his singular persona, Moses illustrates the power of prayer. At Israel's lowest moments, whether dancing around the calf in the desert or living in exile, people reading this psalm demand that the God-Israel relationship continue.

This audacious psalm signals a change in the direction of the book of Psalms. Psalm 91 expresses deep faith in God's protection.

> O you who dwell in the shelter of the Most High and abide in the protection of Shaddai – I say of the Lord, my refuge and stronghold, my God in whom I trust, that He will save you from the fowler's trap, from the destructive plague… (Psalm 91:1–3).

Remarkably, God responds at the end of the psalm:

> Because he is devoted to Me I will deliver him; I will keep him safe, for he knows My name. When he calls on Me, I will answer him; I will be with him in distress; I will rescue him and make him honored; I will let him live to a ripe old age, and show him My salvation (Psalm 91:14–16).

God's responding is extremely unusual in the book of Psalms, which generally reflects people's prayers directed toward God. God's dramatic rejoinder offers breathtaking encouragement to a degraded Israel. When Israel places its faith in God, God lets Israel know that He still is with her in exile. Israel is never alone. Rabbi Shimon b. Yohai poignantly expresses this idea, "Come and see how beloved are Israel in the sight of God, in that to every place to which they were exiled the Shechinah went with them" (*Megillah* 29a).

Psalms 92 and 94 then revitalize the belief in God's ultimate fairness after Psalm 73 had destabilized it:

> I was a dolt, without knowledge (*va-ani ba'ar ve-lo eda*); I was brutish toward You (Psalm 73:22).

> A brutish man cannot know, a fool cannot understand this (*ish ba'ar lo yeda, u-kesil lo yavin et zot*): though the wicked sprout like grass, though all evildoers blossom, it is only that they may be destroyed forever (Psalm 92:7–8).

> Take heed, you most brutish people; fools, when will you get wisdom (*binu bo'arim ba-am, u-kesilim matai taskilu*)? Shall He who implants the ear not hear, He who forms the eye not see? Shall He who disciplines nations not punish, He who instructs men in knowledge? Happy is the man whom You discipline, O Lord, the man You instruct in Your teaching (Psalm 94:8–12).

These psalms return to the position of Psalm 1 and others, that God is fair and even when there is apparent injustice one need only be patient because justice will be served. Psalm 94 stands out in the book of Psalms by introducing the idea of suffering as a sign of divine love. Whereas the psalmist of 73 felt like a fool for doubting God before regaining his faith, the psalmist in 92 criticizes such doubters as fools, and the psalmist in 94 lashes out against them.[3] Faith in God's ultimate fairness has been restored.

The final two psalms in book 4 (105–106) are historical surveys. Each has a common theme relevant to the period of the exile. Psalm 105 speaks of God's eternal promise of the Land of Israel to the Patriarchs. It then surveys how God has always protected our nation while in exile:

The Patriarchs in foreign lands (vv. 12–15), Joseph (vv. 16–22) and then the Israelites in Egypt (vv. 23–38), and the Israelites in the wilderness (vv. 39–41). The psalm concludes that God always remembers the Patriarchal covenant, will give the Land to Israel to their descendants, and in turn expects them to be faithful to the Torah:

> Mindful of His sacred promise to His servant Abraham, He led His people out in gladness, His chosen ones with joyous song. He gave them the lands of nations; they inherited the wealth of peoples, that they might keep His laws and observe His teachings. Hallelujah (Psalm 105:42–45).

Nahum Sarna suggests that this psalm was likely composed in the Babylonian exile. The psalmist appeals to God's past acts throughout history of protecting Israel while in exile. He prays that just as God protected them in the past, so too should He protect their descendants currently in exile. Just as God redeemed the Israelites from Egypt and gave them the Land that He promised to the Patriarchs, so too He should do that for their descendants now. The psalmist also encourages Jews to be faithful to the Torah since the God-Israel covenant must be mutually honored.[4]

Sarna explains that Psalm 106 utilizes the same technique of a historical survey as Psalm 105, albeit with a different vantage point. The psalmist refers to historical instances in which God was good to Israel, yet Israel was unfaithful. God wanted to destroy Israel in the past because of its sins, but refrained from doing so for His Name's sake and because individuals prayed on their behalf. The lesson to glean from this history is that Israel has sinned and therefore is suffering. However, God preserves Israel for His Name's sake and therefore one should pray since God has been responsive to prayer in the past. Drawing the proper lesson from his historical survey, the psalmist concludes with a prayer for redemption:

> He saved them time and again, but they were deliberately rebellious, and so they were brought low by their iniquity. When He saw that they were in distress, when He heard their cry, He was

mindful of His covenant and in His great faithfulness relented. He made all their captors kindly disposed toward them.

Deliver us, O Lord our God, and gather us from among the nations, to acclaim Your holy name, to glory in Your praise. Blessed is the Lord, God of Israel, From eternity to eternity. Let all the people say, "Amen." Hallelujah (Psalm 106:43–48).[5]

Book 4 has stabilized concerns about God's fairness and expresses confidence that God will protect the Jews, redeem them, and return them to their Land as He has done in the past.

Book 5 opens with a celebratory reflection on the return from exile:

"Praise the Lord, for He is good; His steadfast love is eternal!" Thus let the redeemed of the Lord say, those He redeemed from adversity, whom He gathered in from the lands, from east and west, from the north and from the sea (Psalm 107:1–3).

Although not every psalm in book 5 is joyous (see, e.g., Psalms 109 and 137), the overall tone of the book is positive insofar as there are many praises and Hallelujahs to complete the book of Psalms.

Although there is no way to demonstrate that the thematic order of the psalms was intended by the editors of Psalms, it is possible to suggest a progression. Books 1–2 open with a stable confidence in both divine justice and God's covenant with the Davidic dynasty. Book 3 then challenges both of these assertions. Book 4 opens with the powerful voice of Moses, who demands that God should end the nation's suffering. God responds in the following psalm that He is indeed with Israel in their troubles since they have trusted Him. Book 4 goes on to affirm divine justice and to derive lessons from history that God always has protected Israel while in exile, has promised the Jews the Land of Israel, and that Israel has sinned but always can repent and pray. The hope generated from book 4 spills into book 5 which opens with a psalm of gratitude to God for redeeming the exiles and returning them to their land.

Rabbi Elhanan Samet[6] contributes to this discussion by interpreting Psalm 107 as an independent unit and then in its context juxtaposed with 105 and 106. In a vacuum, Psalm 107 teaches that when an individual is in danger, he or she should pray to God, God will save the individual, and then should thank God after being saved. This psalm forms the foundation for the rabbinic blessing, *birkat ha-gomel*, that one recites after surviving dangerous experiences (*Berakhot* 54b).

Contextually, Psalm 107 is the third of a trilogy (105–106–107) of psalms that begin, Praise the Lord (*hodu la-Hashem*). As a trilogy, the psalms encompass all of Israel's history, from Abraham through the final redemption. The historical time in which the author of Psalm 106 is found, and from which he surveys the past history of his people, is the time of the Babylonian exile. The psalmist prays for the ingathering of exiles so that they may give thanks to God.

This psalm is immediately followed by the beginning of 107, which describes how the two elements of this request on the part of the petitioner will be fulfilled in the future:

> "Praise the Lord, for He is good; His steadfast love is eternal!" Thus let the redeemed of the Lord say, those He redeemed from adversity, whom He gathered in from the lands, from east and west, from the north and from the sea (Psalm 107:1–3).

It appears that the barrier that the redactors created between books 4–5 in Psalms is intentional, and that this division stems from their objective to create a fundamental distinction between 105–106 and 107. 105–106 are historical psalms relating to the past, whereas 107 describes the future.

Rabbi Samet argues further that this interpretation is not the entire story. In the future, when the time of redemption will arrive, the people of Israel will repair what they had perverted throughout their history, and they will thank God for the acts of loving kindness that He performed for them. The contrast between 107 and the two preceding psalms is expressed in opening common to all three psalms: "Give thanks to the Lord," at the beginning of 105–106 are the words of the psalmist to Israel, and it is a demand that was never realized. The failure to fulfill this demand lies at the root of all the evil performed by Israel and all the evil that befell them. In contrast, "Give thanks to the Lord," at the beginning of 107 is a citation of the words of the redeemed, and through it the original demand is realized.

As an independent psalm detached from its context, 107 serves as a universal didactic psalm, teaching about the obligation to thank God falling upon any person meriting God's rescue from danger. A consecutive reading of 105, 106, and 107 reveals a dramatically different understanding: it is not a universal psalm, but rather an Israelite psalm that deals with the future history of the people of Israel in contrast to its past history. This psalm of redemption propels us into book 5, with all three Hallels, conveying the ultimate joyous tone.

As individual psalms can change in meaning with time and also have the power to transform those who recite them; so too the entire book of Psalms goes through a process of transition, bringing readers on a journey from a stable world, to instability, and then provides mechanisms for encouraging repentance, faith, and hope. The journey from a simple faith to a more profound and deeper understanding of the God-human relationship leads to the religious ecstasy found in the joyous psalms that are concentrated toward the end of the book.

NOTES

1. For a similar approach to this section in Psalms, see Sampson S. Ndoga, "Revisiting the Theocratic Agenda of Book 4 of the Psalter for Interpretive Premise," in *The Shape and Shaping of the Book of Psalms: The Current State of Scholarship*, ed. Nancy L. deClaisse-Walford (Atlanta: SBL Press, 2014), pp. 147–159.
2. "A Psalm of Moses" could ascribe the psalm to Moses. Alternatively, a later psalmist used Moses' name because he invokes the prophet's brazen terminology and therefore dedicates the psalm to Moses. Rambam suggests that Moses composed Psalm 90 in prophetic anticipation of the exile, and David included it in Psalms to offer comfort and consolation (*Epistle of Consolation*, in Joel Kraemer, *Maimonides: The Life and World of One of Civilization's Greatest Minds*, 2008, p. 12).
3. Francis I. Andersen (*Habakkuk*: Anchor Bible, p. 133) observes that there are no instances in Tanakh where God rebuked someone for questioning God's justice. In the book of Job, God criticized Job's shortsightedness but vindicated his justness as well. It is worth noting that one psalmist does rebuke those who question God's ways (Psalm 94:8–10), and that type of rebuke is unique in Psalms.
4. Nahum M. Sarna, et al., *Olam HaTanakh: Psalms* vol. 2 (Hebrew) (Tel Aviv: Dodson-Iti, 1999), p. 129.
5. See Sarna, et al., *Olam HaTanakh: Psalms* vol. 2, p. 133.
6. At http://vbm-torah.org/archive/tehillim70/57tehillim.htm.

Psalm 104: Interpretation of the Creation Narratives in Genesis

Throughout the ages, commentators have grappled with the two Creation narratives in the first two chapters of Genesis. Is the latter a recapitulation of the Creation or a record of a later incident? Should these chapters be taken literally or as expressions of profound truths? Are there alternatives to these two possibilities?

In this essay, we present three classical approaches to this issue, then a fourth, based on Psalm 104.

TEXTUAL DISCREPANCIES

Chapter one outlines a fairly symmetrical six-day process during which the aspects of the universe were created. At the outset, the earth is covered with water and wind. God creates light and darkness and a firmament between the upper and lower waters, and then separates land from water. Next, God brings forth foliage and the heavenly orbs. Finally, God fashions the sea creatures and birds, then animals and

---

This essay is adapted from my article, "The Psalmist as an Exegete," in Angel, *Through an Opaque Lens*, revised second edition (New York: Kodesh Press, 2013), pp. 75-86.

humankind. This account concludes early in chapter two when God halts Creation on the seventh day.

Aside from this reference to the seventh day, chapter two makes no mention of the six days of Creation. It confines itself to "…the day God the Lord made earth and heaven" (Genesis 2:4).

Instead of the water-covered earth of chapter one, chapter 2 depicts the world as dry and lifeless. A mysterious mist rises from the ground, moisturizing the parched planet.

God fashions man out of dirt, then plants the Garden of Eden and places man there. He subsequently enjoins Adam not to partake of the Tree of Knowledge. Only then does God create wildlife. He concludes creation by sculpting woman from one of Adam's ribs. The order of these creations differs from that in chapter one, where man was created last, not first.

The creation of plants differs in the two chapters as well. In chapter one, God commands the earth to produce all manner of plant life. In chapter two, however, the earth cannot sustain plants without rain or human exertion. God sows the Garden of Eden. Only trees appear to be in the Garden, and only man is to eat of them.

Regarding the beginnings of humankind, chapter one indicates that man and woman were created concurrently. Chapter two separates their creation and emphasizes that woman was constructed from the body of man. Also, the initial creation of man is poetic, with "let us make man" and with humanity formed in the divine image (Genesis 1:26). In contrast, the Garden of Eden narrative portrays man as humbly created from the dirt. God later reminds Adam of these ignoble origins, foretelling his eventual death and return to the earth from which he has come (Genesis 3:19).

God is called by the generic title Elokim (God) in chapter one, whereas He is Hashem Elokim (the Lord God) throughout chapters two and three.

These are the major discrepancies that concern most commentators.[1] We now consider how the exegetes have addressed these issues.

THREE CLASSICAL APPROACHES

Chapter Two Is a Detailed Version of Chapter One
As formulated by Rabbi Eliezer b. Yosei ha-Gelili, one of the 32 hermeneutical principles used to expound the Torah states that when "A general statement [is] followed by an incident, [the latter] is an illustration of the former." Based on this dictum, Rashi and many others view the creation of man in the second chapter as a detailing of the first chapter.[2] Chapter two, then, occurs on the sixth day of creation.[3]

Those who adopt this approach must harmonize the apparent incongruities between the two chapters. Several commentators impose the particulars of chapter two onto the more general chapter one (particularly regarding the creation of man) and the chronology of chapter one onto chapter two.

For instance, because the latter refers only to "the *day* God the Lord made earth and heaven" (Genesis 2:4), some conclude that Creation occurred *in one day*, after which – as noted in chapter one – God fashioned what had been created.[4] Alternatively, Radak suggests that heaven and earth were created on the first day, but that the rest of creation occurred over the next five days. He maintains that the separation of sea and land took place on the *first* day, despite its mention on the third day. Thus, he reads the verse, "God said: Let the waters… be gathered…" (Genesis 1:9), as a pluperfect, "God *had* said."

To explain the fact that man is created *after* plants and animals in chapter one, but before them in chapter two, most commentators interpret the conversive *vavs* in verses 2:8–9 and 2:19 in the pluperfect, i.e., "God the Lord *had* planted a garden in Eden…," "God the Lord *had* brought forth from the ground every tree…," and "God the Lord *had* fashioned from the ground every beast of the field…," all before "God the Lord created man…" (Genesis 2:7). Following midrashic precedents, Rashi writes that the plants created on the third day waited underground until man emerged and prayed for rain. Similarly, Radak and Malbim state that even after "…a mist arose…and watered the whole face of the ground" (Genesis 2:6), only wild plants sprang up. Grain did not grow until man was created and helped to cultivate it.[5]

Several proponents of the approach under discussion assert that chapter one summarizes the creation of humans in general, while chapter two specifies the creation of Adam and Eve.[6] Radak and Malbim (on Genesis 1:27) maintain that chapter one (where *bara* is used) describes the spiritual creation of man, whereas chapter two (where *yatzar* appears) depicts his physical formation.

All these exegetes need not address chapter two's failure to mention water and its life forms, which are immaterial to the chapter's focus on humans.

Finally, regarding God's different names, Ibn Ezra quotes a Midrash which states that "Hashem" was added to "Elokim" only after the world was complete, since "Hashem Elokim" is God's complete Name.[7]

B. *The Creation Account Has Hidden Meaning*

Ramban and Rambam both posit that the text contains the esoteric secrets of Creation and therefore should not be understood literally. Ramban (on Genesis 1:1) states that the Creation narratives are beyond our ken and exist only to establish that God created the world. As for the mysteries of the Creation process, he adds (on Genesis 1:6) that it is forbidden to reveal them.

Similarly, Rambam maintains that the true meaning of Creation should remain hidden from those ignorant of metaphysics:

> Not everything in the Torah concerning the Account of the Beginning is to be taken in its external sense as the vulgar imagine. For if the matter were such, the men of knowledge would not have been chary of divulging knowledge with regard to it, and the Sages would not have expatiated on its being kept secret and on preventing the talk about it in the presence of the vulgar.[8] For the external sense of these texts leads either to a grave corruption of the imagination and to giving vent to the evil opinions with regard to the Deity, or to an absolute denial of the action of the deity and to disbelief in the foundations of the law.... It is obligatory to consider them with what is truly the intellect after one has acquired perfection in the demonstrative sciences and knowledge of the secrets of the

prophets. However...none of those who know something of it should divulge it.... [It is] forbidden to be explicit about it (*Guide* 2:29).⁹

C. Chapter Two Follows Chapter One Chronologically
Sforno (on Genesis 2:4) submits a third approach. In chapter one, God created only potential. However, nothing became actualized until chapter two and the advent of man, after the six days of Creation. According to Sforno, the two chapters do not conflict, since chapter two chronologically follows chapter one.

For example, on the third day of creation, in chapter one, God enriched the earth with nutrients to sustain plant life, but nothing sprouted until 2:8, after man was already created in 2:7. Thus, Sforno need not interpret the conversive *vavs* of verses 2:8 and 2:19 in the pluperfect (as discussed above), for plants and animals did not physically exist until after the creation of man.

Sforno's view is most striking in his explanation that man was placed in the Garden of Eden in chapter two in order to develop the divine image with which he was created in chapter one.¹⁰

Sforno (on Genesis 2:4) explains the variation in God's Names by contending that the Tetragrammaton could be used only after the six days of creation established a permanent pattern of time in this world, since this appellation incorporates the element of time in God's name: "was," "is," and "will be."

PSALM 104: A KEY TO UNDERSTANDING GENESIS 1–2

A. The Purpose of the World

> In the Torah, Moses recorded many actions in an obscure manner, but David came and explained them. We find in the creation account that after God created heavens and the earth, He created light, as it is written (Genesis 1:1, 3), "In the beginning, God created [the heavens and the earth]," and afterwards, "and God said, 'Let there be light.'" David explained that after God created light, He created heavens, as it is written (Psalm

104:2), "wrapped in a robe of light," and only afterwards, "You spread the heavens like a tent cloth." We may derive from here that after God created light, He created heavens (*Exodus Rabbah* 15:22).[11]

This Midrash views the composer of Psalm 104 as the first "exegete" to grapple with the two accounts of creation. Let us consider how the Psalm presents the formation of the world:

> Bless the Lord, O my soul; O Lord, my God, You are very great; You are clothed in glory and majesty, wrapped in a robe of light; You spread the heavens like a tent cloth.... You made the deep cover it as a garment; the waters stood above the mountains. They fled at Your blast, rushed away at the sound of Your thunder – mountains rising, valleys sinking – to the place You established for them. You set bounds they must not pass so that they never again cover the earth (Psalm 104:1–9).

The psalmist mentions light (created on day one of Creation), then the heavens (day two), and then the separation of water from land (day three). Thus far, he mirrors the sequence of Genesis 1. Then the Psalm becomes more complex:

> You make springs gush forth in torrents; they make their way between the hills, giving drink to all the wild beasts; the wild asses slake their thirst. The birds of the sky dwell beside them and sing among the foliage. You water the mountains from Your lofts; the earth is sated from the fruit of Your work. You make the grass grow for the cattle, and herbage for man's labor that he may get food out of the earth – wine that cheers the hearts of men oil that makes the face shine, and bread that sustains man's life. The trees of the Lord drink their fill, the cedars of Lebanon, His own planting, where birds make their nests; the stork has her home in the junipers. The high mountains are for wild goats; the crags are a refuge for rock-badgers (Psalm 104:10–18).

As the psalmist describes the creation of springs as well as trees and other vegetation (day three), he specifies their purpose: to feed and shelter birds (created on the fifth day) and animals and humans (created on the sixth). He maintains the order of Creation; however, by inserting the function of everything to serve all sentient creatures, he redefines the very acts of creation.

The Psalm then moves into the fourth day of creation:

> He made the moon to mark the seasons; the sun knows when to set. You bring on darkness and it is night, when all the beasts of the forests stir. The lions roar for prey, seeking their food from God. When the sun rises, they come home and couch in their dens. Man then goes out to his work, to his labor until the evening (Psalm 104:20–23).

The celestial bodies govern the life cycle. When the moon appears, nocturnal beasts emerge; when the sun rises, these creatures return home, while humans awaken and work until sunset. Once again, the psalmist focuses on how inanimate creations benefit living beings, both human and animal.

To summarize, the opening 23 verses of Psalm 104 recount in order the first four days of Creation, citing the creations of the fifth and sixth days as the reason everything else was created. The psalmist begins and ends this section by praising God, the Omnipotent Creator. As Radak writes (on Psalm 104:1), "This Psalm relates the creation account and that God has in His wisdom made all creations for the benefit of [living] creatures."

Equipped with this understanding of Psalm 104, let us return to Genesis 1–2.

B. Anthropocentrism

A cursory reading of the two creation accounts suggests that Genesis 1 is theocentric, while Genesis 2 revolves around Adam and the Garden of Eden. Thus, Psalm 104 resembles Genesis 2 in highlighting that the world was created for people, but also adheres to the sequence of Genesis 1. However, a closer look at Genesis 1 reveals that it too has anthropocentric leanings.

As noted, in Genesis 1, God creates plants on the third day, whereas, in Genesis 2, plants appear only after Adam. We have seen how different commentators resolve this difficulty. Yet Genesis 1 concludes with a new insight:

> God said, "See, I give you every seed-bearing plant that is upon all the earth, and every tree that has seed-bearing fruit; they shall be yours for food. And to all the animals on land, to all the birds of the sky, and to everything that creeps on earth, in which there is the breath of life, [I give] all the green plants for food." And it was so (Genesis 1:29–30).

When God plants the Garden of Eden and instructs Adam "...to till it and to tend it" (Genesis 2:15), this directive parallels the above passage, not the creation of foliage on the third day. According to both Genesis 2 and the end of Genesis 1, the purpose of the vegetation is to nourish living beings. This interpretation is consistent with the psalmist's.

Moreover, Genesis states of the great heavenly lights:

> God said, "Let there be lights in the expanse of the sky to separate day from night; they shall serve as signs for the set times – the days and the years" (Genesis 1:14).

Even in the "objective" creation account, the function of the sun, moon, and stars is to mark times, relevant only to humanity. Likewise, they are created "to separate between light and the darkness" (Genesis 1:18), benefiting both man and animals in their working and hunting schedules. This interpretation too conforms to Psalm 104.

Additionally, Genesis 1 clearly agrees with both Genesis 2 and Psalm 104 that the world was created primarily for people:

> And God said, "Let us make man in our image, after our likeness. They shall rule the fish of the sea, the birds of the sky, the cattle, the whole earth, and all the creeping things that creep on earth" (Genesis 1:26).

This blessing begins its fulfillment in Genesis 2:19–20, where man asserts his dominion over animals by naming them.

Thus, the two creation accounts are in fact similar thematically.

Chapter 1 maintains the objective sequence of Creation and underscores its purpose: to serve living beings, mainly people. Chapter 2 deviates from this chronological order, placing man in the center of Creation.

Psalm 104 unifies the two chapters by preserving the chronology of Genesis 1 and the anthropocentrism of Genesis 2.

C. "Bless God, O My Soul"

Thus far, the psalmist has equated man and animals. The springs, plants, and lights benefit both equally. The psalmist now shifts his focus:

> How many are the things You have made, O Lord; You have made them all with wisdom; the earth is full of Your creations. There is the sea, vast and wide, with its creatures beyond number, living things, small and great. There go the ships, and Leviathan that You formed to sport with. All of them look to You to give them their food when it is due. Give it to them, they gather it up; open Your hand, they are well satisfied; hide Your face, they are terrified; take away their breath, they perish and turn again into dust; send back Your breath, they are created, and You renew the face of the earth (Psalm 104:24–30).

After praising God's creation, the Psalm proclaims that all creations depend on Him for sustenance. Although God created the world to benefit living creatures, they must recognize their reliance on their Creator. On the one hand, Psalm 104 is far more "democratic" than Genesis, as animals benefit from inanimate creation as much as humans. However, only man has the awareness that he benefits from God's creation. The psalmist therefore concludes on a distinctly human note[12]:

> I will sing to the Lord as long as I live; all my life I will chant hymns to my God. May my prayer be pleasing to Him; I will rejoice in the Lord. May sinners disappear from the earth, and the wicked be no more.[13] Bless the Lord, O my soul. Hallelujah[14] (Psalm 104:33–35).

Thus, the Psalm begins and ends with the uniquely human capability of apprehending God through nature and seeking a relationship with Him as a result. As Radak (on Psalm 104:1) observes, "the psalmist says, 'Bless God, O my soul…' since no living being knows how to praise God except man, who has intellect."[15]

CONCLUSION

Psalm 104 combines the sequence of Genesis 1 with the message that the world was created for living beings, primarily humans. By studying Genesis 1–2 and Psalm 104 together, we find a thread connecting all three passages, highlighting man's purpose.

Psalm 104 concludes that, although the world was given to all creatures, man has a special obligation to see God's hand in the creation and accordingly pursue spirituality. As Rambam writes:

> What is the path to achieving love and fear [of God]? When a man contemplates His wondrous and great doings and creations, and he realizes [God's] wisdom is infinite, immediately he will love and extol and exalt and feel great pangs to know the Great God… (*Hilkhot Yesodei ha-Torah* 2:2).

NOTES

1. The language of creation used in the two accounts is also dissimilar. In chapter one, God creates with the verbs *bara* (used exclusively in divine creation) and *asah* simply by speaking (e.g., "The Lord said: Let there be light…" Genesis 1:3). This terminology suggests a mighty God capable of creating in a Godly way. As one Midrash suggests, God can create by merely declaring, while a person can only *fashion* what he is given (see *Midrash Psalms* 18, cited in *Torah Shelemah* [Kasher], vol. 1, p. 178. Also see *Genesis Rabbah* 1:9, in which a philosopher challenges *creatio ex nihilo*, stating that God used primeval *tohu va-vohu*, darkness, wind, and water to fashion the rest of creation. Rabban Gamliel responds that each of these substances appears elsewhere in the Bible alongside the verb *bara*, indicating that God created them as well.) Ironically, the main creative verb in chapter two is *yatzar* (see Genesis 2:7, 8, 19; interestingly, Onkelos translates *yatzar* as *bara*). When God forms woman, the Torah uses *banah*, "build" (Genesis 2:22).
2. See Rashi on Genesis 2:8 and, for example, Radak on Genesis 2:6.
3. See Rashbam, Radak on Genesis 1:27.
4. *Genesis Rabbah* 1:19 maintains that, on the first day, "God created the heavens and the earth" (Genesis 1:1), including the orbs in the sky and all life on earth. Similarly, Hizkuni (on Genesis 1:1, 3) states that, on day one, only land, sky, and light were created. These things subsequently "became pregnant" and produced the other creations on the other days.

    In contrast, Ibn Ezra (on Genesis 2:4) argues that the elements had the power to produce starting from the first day, yet the world was created in six days. See *Torah Shelemah*, vol. 1, ns. 205, 236, and 358; Rashi on Genesis 1:14, and *Or ha-Hayyim* and Malbim on Genesis 1:1. Ramban (on Genesis 1:1) and Sforno (on Genesis 1:2) state that God first created *tohu va-vohu*, and from this raw material He fashioned everything created during the six days. These commentators generally contend that *bara* means *creatio ex nihilo* whereas *asah* pertains to the fashioning of existing matter. Sforno (on Genesis 1:16, 21; 2:4) agrees that everything happened on the first day, but he assumes that the creation depicted in chapter one did not become physical reality until man was formed. We discuss his position later in this essay.

    Others insist that the world was indeed created in six days that the "the *day* God the Lord made earth and heaven" (Genesis 2:4) refers to this entire period. See *Torah Shelemah*, vol. 1, ns. 205 and 634; the latter associates *asah* with miraculous creation. Also see Rabbi Saadiah Gaon (on Genesis 2:4) and Ibn Ezra (on Genesis 1:1).

    Malbim (on Genesis 1:1) connects this dispute with the question of how to understand Genesis 1:1–3. According to Rashi, Ibn Ezra, and Ralbag, the verses read: "In the beginning of God's creation of the heavens and the earth… God said: Let there be light." In other words, light was the first creation in the six-day process of creating heaven and earth. However, for Radak, Ramban, and Malbim, the verses read: "In the beginning, God created the heavens and the earth…. God said: Let there be light." According to this reading, heaven and earth were the first creations, and the next five days involved fashioning these materials into the rest of creation.

5. See Radak and Malbim on Genesis 2:5–6. From the phrase "And *every* plant of the field was not yet in the earth, because… there was no man to work the ground" (Genesis 2:5), Malbim deduces that *some* species already existed, having been created on the third day. "*Every* plant" did not, however, for those requiring human sowing or rain (which hinges on God's supervision of people). These species waited until after man was created.

6. See, for example, Rashi on Genesis 1:27, 2:21.

7. See *Genesis Rabbah* 13:3, Ibn Ezra on Genesis 2:14.

8. See *Genesis Rabbah* 9:1.

9. Translation of Shlomo Pines (Chicago: University of Chicago Press, 1963), pp. 346–347.

10. Cf. *Genesis Rabbah* 14:1. Or ha-Hayyim (2:5) quotes a parallel idea that man activates the world. For further discussion of Sforno's interpretation in light of broader themes in his commentary, see Hayyim Angel, "Text and Historical Motivations Behind the Commentary of Rabbi Ovadiah Sforno on the Torah," in Angel, *Peshat Isn't So Simple: Essays on Developing a Religious Methodology to Bible Study* (New York: Kodesh Press, 2014), pp. 105–117.

11. Based on this Midrash, Rashi, Ibn Ezra, and Ralbag maintain that light was created before heaven and earth. Radak, Ramban, Hizkuni, and Malbim, argue the opposite, however, adopting the view of Rabbi Nehemiah (as opposed to Rabbi Judah) in *Genesis Rabbah* 3:1.

12. Rabbi Joseph B. Soloveitchik observes that "You will not find in the Bible any song that does not culminate in ethical conclusions. Even the most sublime hymn on the beauty and splendor ends with a moral judgment: 'I will sing praise to my God while I live… I will rejoice in the Lord. Let sinners depart from the earth, and the wicked are no more. Let my soul bless God, Halleluiah' (Ps. 104:33–35)" (in *Worship of the Heart*, ed. Shalom Carmy [Hoboken, NJ: Ktav, 2003], p. 159).

13. The jarring appearance of this petition at the conclusion of the Psalm reminds us that there is another trait unique to humanity: our ability to do evil. The psalmist's pure joy in God and creation is shaken by the existence of human evil, so he prays for their destruction so that his portrayal of God's masterpiece of Creation will be complete.

14. This is the first time the word "Hallelujah" appears in the book of Psalms. There is an ancient debate whether this word should be the last word of a psalm, or whether it is the first word of the next psalm (see *Pesahim* 117a). In the Septuagint, "Hallelujah" is placed at the beginning of the psalm, except for Psalm 150 where it is the last word of the book. The Masoretes placed them at the end of the psalms, but they wrote the word on a separate line, perhaps preserving this sense of doubt. In the MT, ten psalms begin with "Hallelujah": 106, 111–113, 135, 146–150.
15. Radak's interpretation is plausible, but it is not compelling. The psalm may be focusing on God's beneficence to all creation, rather than making a point to distinguish between the reactions of humans and animals.

Psalms 113–118:
Hallel

We often refer to Psalms 113–118 recited on holidays as "the Egyptian *Hallel*" (*Berakhot* 56a), reflecting the content of Psalm 114 that refers explicitly to "When Israel went forth from Egypt." In this essay, we will explore two of the psalms in that unit, 113 and 117.

PSALM 113

Hallelujah. O servants of the Lord, give praise; praise the name of the Lord. Let the name of the Lord be blessed now and forever. From east to west the name of the Lord is praised. The Lord is exalted above all nations; His glory is above the heavens. Who is like the Lord our God, who, enthroned on high, sees what is below, in heaven and on earth? He raises the poor from the dust, lifts up the needy from the refuse heap to set them with the great, with the great men of His people. He sets the childless woman among her household as a happy mother of children. Hallelujah.

Rabbi Elhanan Samet[1] observes that the first half of the psalm (verses 1–4) reflects praise of God as infinite in all realms. The second half transitions after "Who is like the Lord our God" in verse 5. The psalmist now describes God acting benevolently in the human arena, specifically helping the downtrodden. God is not high and mighty like human kings, but rather comes down to the people to see and help them.

In the first half of the psalm, God's name appears five times, and there are five words of praise. In the second half, God's name is mentioned only at the transition, and there are no words of praise. By saying *"our* God" in verse five, the congregation feels an intimate relationship with God, and this signals the transition in the psalm to God's relationship with people. The second half of the psalm focuses on God's concern for the downtrodden and how He raises them up. This attribute is at the root of God's humility. Rabbi Samet quotes *Megillah* 31a: "Wherever you find [a reference in the Bible to] the might of the Holy One, Blessed be He, you find [a reference to] His humility [adjacent to it]."

PSALM 117

Praise the Lord, all you nations; extol Him, all you peoples, for great is His steadfast love towards us; the faithfulness of the Lord endures forever. Hallelujah.

Consisting of only two verses, Psalm 117 is the shortest chapter in Tanakh.[2] This succinct prayer contains a message dear to all committed Jews: not only do we long for fellow Jews to develop a religious connection with our Creator, but we also anticipate the day when all people of the world recognize God as the Master of the Universe.

Yet, a difficulty arises in understanding our Psalm. Why should Gentiles praise God because He has been steadfastly good *to Israel*? Why would the psalmist employ such a seemingly nonessential reason to draw people closer to God? Among our commentators, there is a wide range of opinions.

MIDRASHIC RESPONSES: MULTIPLE VOICES

"Praise the Lord, all you nations": Why should the nations of the world do this (Rashi: to praise God for His steadfast love towards us – *we* should praise Him)? Understand it this way: "Praise the Lord, all you nations" – for the great acts and wonders which God does for *them* [i.e., the nations]; how much more should we [Israel], for great is His steadfast love towards us (*Pesahim* 118b).

This midrashic reading divides the Psalm into different voices. The first verse is a call from the psalmist to Gentiles to praise God. In contrast, the second verse suddenly has Israel introspectively realizing their own duty to express gratitude for their special relationship with their Creator. Rashi appears to adopt this reading, as well.

In *Midrash Psalms* 117:2, we find a similar line of reasoning, that our psalm also addresses Israel's relationship with God. This Midrash breaks our psalm into three different voices, instead of only two:

> Rabbi Shimon, son of our Holy Rabbi, asked his father, "who are the 'nations,' and who are the 'peoples'?" He replied, "'all you nations' refers to those nations who have enslaved Israel; 'all you peoples' refers to those peoples who did not enslave them. The [latter] peoples said, if those nations who enslaved Israel are praising God, how much more so must we, who have not enslaved Israel....
>
> [Upon hearing this,] Israel said, [if so,] we should praise God even more! They began to say 'for great is His steadfast love towards us.'"

According to this midrashic reading, the nations who have oppressed Israel (*goyim*) begin to praise God. This leads those nations more benevolent to Israel (*ha-ummim*) to join in the praises. Finally, Israel (*ki gavar alenu hasdo*) recognizes God's unique relationship with them, and they realize how much more they are obliged to glorify God.

Both rabbinic passages belong to the realm of *derash*. By inserting critical clauses into the flow, they poignantly illustrate the difficulty of this short psalm. We will now consider the *peshat* commentators, to see how they contend with our psalm.

RADAK: ANTICIPATING MESSIANIC TIMES

Radak maintains that this psalm speaks of the messianic era, when all nations will embrace God. In the future, Gentiles will praise God because they see how unfailing He has been in fulfilling His pledge of beneficence to Israel. Until that point, Gentiles found it difficult to believe in God's justice, since Israel was suffering. When they see Israel's redemption, the nations will be so impressed that they will gravitate towards serving God.

AMOS HAKHAM: *KIDDUSH HASHEM* AND *HILLUL HASHEM*

Amos Hakham offers a different interpretation of our psalm.[3] A recurring theme in the Bible is the desire that all humanity will serve God. However, it is easier to see the hand of God when righteous people are successful. When the righteous suffer, many deny God's Providence. Hakham cites Psalm 115:1–2, which describes the opposite phenomenon of our psalm:

> Not to us, O Lord, not to us but to Your Name bring glory for the sake of Your love and Your faithfulness. Let the nations not say, "Where, now, is their God?"

Psalm 66:8–9 is conceptually similar to Psalm 117:

> O peoples, bless our God, celebrate His praises; who has granted us life, and has not let our feet slip.

Hakham also cites Ezekiel 36:22–23:

> Thus said the Lord God: Not for your sake will I act, O House of Israel, but for my holy Name, which you have caused to be profaned among the nations to which you have come. I will sanctify My great Name which has been profaned among the nations.…And the nations shall know that I am the Lord… when I manifest My holiness before their eyes through you.

Hakham argues that our psalm should be taken literally. The nations should praise God because He has been good to Israel. Israel's thriving will inspire the nations to pursue a closer association with God.

Yehezkel Kaufmann[4] adds that the concept that Gentile nations should praise God because of God's goodness to Israel is common in the book of Psalms. For example:

> He was mindful of His steadfast love and faithfulness toward the house of Israel; all the ends of the earth beheld the victory of our God. Raise a shout to the Lord, all the earth, break into joyous songs of praise! (Psalm 98:3–4).

> A psalm for praise. Raise a shout for the Lord, all the earth; worship the Lord in gladness; come into His presence with shouts of joy. Acknowledge that the Lord is God; He made us and we are His, His people, the flock He tends. Enter His gates with praise, His courts with acclamation. Praise Him! Bless His name! For the Lord is good; His steadfast love is eternal; His faithfulness is for all generations (Psalm 100).

The psalmists expect that Gentiles will praise God because of God's beneficence to Israel.

Adopting a similar reading, Rashbam (on Deuteronomy 32:43) suggests that when non-Jewish nations witness God's kindness to Israel, they are inspired to serve God as well. The psalmist calls on them to serve God so that God will be good to them as He is good to Israel. In Rashbam's reading, non-Jewish nations stand to benefit directly by serving God.

IBN EZRA AND MALBIM: HISTORICAL CONTEXTS

Despite arguing over the fundamental nature of this psalm, Rashi, Radak, and Hakham agree that our psalm addresses *all* nations. This view is supported by the fact that the psalm solicits *kol goyim* and *kol ha-ummim* (*all* you nations, *all* you peoples). In contrast, Ibn Ezra and Malbim explicate our psalm in an historical context, understanding the psalmist at least initially to be addressing specific nations, rather than all Gentiles.

Ibn Ezra attributes our psalm to King David, who had vanquished the surrounding enemy nations. Addressing his new pagan subjects,

King David calls on them to praise God. Ibn Ezra explains the phrase, "the faithfulness of the Lord endures forever" as a directive from David for the nations to abandon their idolatrous beliefs and to espouse belief in the true God.

Although Ibn Ezra does not address our question directly, it would appear that David is entreating the nations in his jurisdiction to exalt God for two reasons: (1) Since God has allowed Israel to overthrow her adversaries, the defeated nations should acknowledge God's omnipotence; (2) since their deities are false, they should forsake them and praise God. The psalm is a triumphant affirmation of God's dominion.

Like Ibn Ezra, Malbim also interprets our psalm in a historical context, addressing a specific group of Gentiles, as opposed to all nations. However, he asserts that this psalm addresses the nations in the time of the Assyrian Empire, centuries after David.[5] During their conquest of the Near East, the Assyrians exiled the Northern tribes of Israel, conquered many other lands, and repopulated countries with peoples of diverse backgrounds (see II Kings 17).

According to Malbim, our psalm petitions specifically those Gentiles who were exiled along with the Israelites. When God liberates the Israelites who had been exiled, those Gentiles who had languished will benefit from Israel's redemption as well. Therefore, they should praise God for His having been good to Israel, since they have gained themselves.

The exegetes we have considered thus far agree that in the phrase *ki gavar alenu hasdo*, "for great is His steadfast love towards *us*," the "us" refers to Israel, and the love God has for us. The Talmud and *Midrash Psalms* cited earlier also read our psalm in this manner. But not all commentators concur on this point.

RABBI MOSHE IBN GIKATILLA: A UNIVERSALIST INTERPRETATION

Rabbi Moshe ibn Gikatilla,[6] quoted by Ibn Ezra on this psalm, asserts that God's steadfast love to "us" refers to the benefits of the entire world (and not just Israel):

And Rabbi Moshe says that it [the phrase, *kol goyim*] includes all nations. The meaning is that steadfast are the acts of lovingkindness which He does with *all*, keeping them alive and sustaining them.

This explanation dramatically alters our understanding of the psalm. According to Ibn Gikatilla, the psalmist calls on the nations of the world to praise God, because they have benefited as *human beings* from God's goodness.[7] It would appear, then, that Ibn Gikatilla would read the psalm this way:

Praise the Lord, all you nations (all nations, including Israel)… *for great is His steadfast love towards us* (all people, including Israel).[8]

This universalist reading of our psalm has midrashic antecedents as well:

When a human king is praised, his supporters come, but his enemies do not. But everyone praises God, as it is written, "all nations whom You have made shall come and prostrate themselves before You, O Lord, and shall glorify Your Name" (Psalm 86:9).

Someone asked Rabbi Joshua b. Hananiah, "on what day is the entire world equal, when all nations bow before God?" He replied, "… when the rains fall, all celebrate and extol God, as it is written, 'all nations whom You have made, etc.' When is this? 'For You are great, and do wondrous things' (Psalm 86:10). And 'wondrous things' refers to rain.… For this reason, it is written 'Praise the Lord, all you nations'" (Psalm 117:1).

Rabbi Tanhum says, "greater is rain from the giving of the Torah, for the Torah made [only] Israel happy, but rain brings joy to the entire world…" (*Midrash Psalms* 117).

This Midrash reflects the vision that all nations should serve God. The focus on the equality of all nations with Israel in praising God is made sharper by Rabbi Tanhum, who considers rainfall even more important (at least in certain ways) than the giving of the Torah. Rainfall benefits all people, whereas the Torah is exclusively for Israel.

From this vantage point, our psalm points to God's universal kindness to the world and calls upon all nations, including Israel, to sing to God for His largesse to "us," all humanity.

Perhaps the most fascinating aspect of this analysis is the fact that a familiar psalm of only two verses contains so many possible interpretations. When one realizes the complexity in the shortest chapter in the Bible, it gives one impetus to probe further into longer sections as well.

NOTES

1. At https://www.etzion.org.il/en/shiur-06-psalm-113-%E2%80%9Cgive-praise-o-servants-lord-praise-name-lord%E2%80%9D-first-psalm-hallel; https://www.etzion.org.il/en/shiur-07-psalm-113-%E2%80%9Cgive-praise-o-servants-lord-praise-name-lord%E2%80%9D-first-psalm-hallel-part-ii.
2. Radak begins his commentary by noting, "this psalm is composed of only two verses." The Aleppo Codex and Leningrad Codex likewise consider the two verses to be the entire psalm. Meiri, on the other hand, connects Psalm 117 with its predecessor, considering them one longer psalm.
3. Amos Hakham, *Da'at Mikra: Psalms* vol. 2 (Hebrew), (Jerusalem: Mosad HaRav Kook, 1979), pp. 362–363.
4. Cited in Feivel Meltzer, *Penei Sefer Tehillim* (Jerusalem: Mossad HaRav Kook, 1982), pp. 332–333.
5. In both his introduction to Psalms as well as his commentary, Malbim ascribes several psalms to authors living after the time of King David, based on their content (e.g., Psalms 53, 89, 137). For discussion of traditional views on the authorship of Psalms, see the introductory chapter in this volume.
6. Rabbi Moshe ibn Gikatilla was born in Cordoba at the beginning of the eleventh century. Rashi and Ibn Ezra regularly quote him, usually referring to him as "Rabbi Moshe," or "Rabbi Moshe ha-Kohen." Ibn Ezra refers to Rabbi Moshe ibn Gikatilla in his own book on grammar, *Moznayim*, as "the greatest of the grammarians," and "one of the great commentators." For a treatment of Rabbi Moshe's commentary on Psalms, see Uriel Simon, *Four Approaches to the Book of Psalms: from Saadiah Gaon to Abraham Ibn Ezra* (Albany: SUNY Press, 1991), pp. 113–144.
7. Rabbi Samson Raphael Hirsch adopts a similar position.
8. Although Radak interprets this particular reference to *goyim* in Psalm 117 as referring to Gentiles, he was well aware of the transition between the biblical usage of *goy* to refer to any nation including Israel, and the rabbinic usage of the term *goy* specifically in reference to Gentiles. See *Sefer ha-Shorashim* 57.

Psalms 121, 126:
Journeys and Redemption

Psalms 120–134 form a group of fifteen psalms that begin *shir ha-ma'alot* (121 begins *la-ma'alot*). Amos Hakham surveys possible meanings of *ma'alot* in that context: (1) Those who go up to Jerusalem on a holiday pilgrimage. (2) Those who returned to Israel from the Babylonian exile. (3) Some, now unknown, musical notation. (4) Mishnah *Middot* 2:5 suggests that there were fifteen steps in the Temple, and perhaps these psalms were recited there.

As a result of the uncertainty surrounding this term, we turn to the contents of each psalm to determine its meaning. In this essay, we will explore two of these psalms, 121 and 126.

PSALM 121

A song for ascents. I turn my eyes to the mountains; from where will my help come? My help comes from the Lord, maker of heaven and earth. He will not let your foot give way; your guardian will not slumber; See, the guardian of Israel neither slumbers nor sleeps! The Lord is your guardian, the Lord is your protection at your right hand. By day the sun will not strike you, nor the moon by night. The Lord will guard you from all harm; He will guard your life. The Lord will guard your going and coming now and forever.

Rabbi Elhanan Samet[1] suggests that the psalm sounds like an individual is setting out on a journey, frightened of potential dangers that await him. Amos Hakham adopts a similar reading.

"I turn my eyes to the mountains" in verse 1 relates the traveler's feelings, anxious about the unknown hazards in the mountains ahead, but assuring himself that God can help him.[2] In essence, this psalm is an early form of *tefillat ha-derekh*, a traveler's prayer for safety. Some versions of the rabbinic *tefillat ha-derekh* include Psalm 121, as well.

Some modern commentaries understand the psalm as having two separate speakers. After the traveler (the first speaker) comforts himself by stating that God will keep the traveler safe (verse 2), another person (the second speaker) blesses him for the duration of the psalm. This second individual speaks from verses 3–8, assuring the traveler that God should indeed protect him from all harm. The exclamation, "See, the guardian of Israel neither slumbers nor sleeps!" (verse 4) could be the words of the traveler (speaker one), interjecting an agreement to the assurances of the second person (Hakham, Samet).

In verse 6, the second person prays that God should protect the traveler from the rays of the sun and the moon, since he will be exposed to those rays more than one who remains at home. In the ancient world, there was a widespread belief that the moon's rays were harmful (see, for example, *Pesahim* 111a, Ibn Ezra, Radak). The term "lunatic" similarly derives from that belief.

The second person concludes his blessing with a broader prayer that God should bless the traveler on this trip and on all future trips.

PSALM 126

A song of ascents. When the Lord restores the fortunes of Zion – we see it as in a dream – our mouths shall be filled with laughter, our tongues, with songs of joy. Then shall they say among the nations, "The Lord has done great things for them!" The Lord will do great things for us and we shall rejoice. Restore our fortunes, O Lord, like watercourses in the Negeb. They who sow in tears shall reap with songs of joy. Though he goes along weeping, carrying the seed-bag, he shall come back with songs of joy, carrying his sheaves.

Psalm 126 appears to refer to the return from the Babylonian exile at the beginning of the Second Temple period. Rashi maintains that it describes the return from Babylonian exile. Alternatively, Malbim suggests that it was written in the Babylonian exile, and it expresses a dream of the future return from that exile.

Rabbi Elhanan Samet[3] offers an analysis of this psalm, surveying the positions of the classical commentators and presenting his interpretation. The following discussion draws from his work.

The term *shivat Tziyon* (verse 1) has been understood as "the captives of Zion," interpreting the word *shivat* as deriving from the root *sh-b-h*, "capture" (Targum, many classical commentators). Several recent scholars tend to favor the root *sh-v-b*, meaning "to return to the original state."[4] Shadal and Rabbi Samet adopt this reading, interpreting the verse "when God redeemed and rehabilitated Zion." In our particular case, the meaning of the verse remains the same: Restoring Israel to its original state means bringing their captives back from exile.

Commentators debate the perspective of the psalm. Has this restoration occurred already, or does the psalmist longingly dream for redemption while still in exile? The terms *hayinu ke-holemim, hayinu semehim* (verses 1, 3) sound like they are in the past tense, but they could be interpreted as we see it in a dream, we shall rejoice (as the NJPS translation above renders these words). In contrast, *az yemmalei, az yomeru* (verse 2) appear to be in the future tense, but they also can be interpreted in an ongoing present tense. Because of these grammatical ambiguities, and because dreams can be pleasant or nightmarish, there are several possibilities.

If the psalm were composed after the return to Israel, the opening verses could mean:

- When we returned to Israel, the redemption felt like a wonderful dream (Ibn Ezra, Radak, Meiri).
- When we returned to Israel, the exile felt like a bad, fleeting nightmare (Radak, Rabbi Yeshayah of Trani).

If the psalm were composed when the people were still in exile, the opening verses could mean:

- When we do return to Israel, it will feel like a good dream (Malbim).
- When we do return to Israel, the exile will feel like it was a nightmare that is now gone (not attested in the commentaries I have consulted).

After surveying the possibilities, Rabbi Samet observes that the prayer in verse 4: "Restore our fortunes, O Lord, like watercourses in the Negeb" suggests that the entire dream has not yet been fulfilled. Something is still lacking. Rabbi Samet attempts to combine the complex possibilities into a composite thesis. Some redemption already has occurred, but there is still more to be done so the psalmist prays for a complete redemption. The Persian Emperor Cyrus granted permission for the Jews to return to Israel and rebuild the Temple. This miracle of history felt like a wonderful dream for the community, and they celebrated joyously. Since other nations destroyed by Babylonia did not return to their homelands, the nations of the world were impressed by the restoration of Israel's fortunes.

Although there was much to celebrate, a majority of the Jews chose to remain in the Babylonian exile. The second half of the psalm is a prayer for the return of the rest of the exiles to the Land of Israel.

Thus, the psalm reflects the complex mood in Israel at the beginning of the Second Temple period. On the one hand, the people were deliriously happy over the miraculous return. On the other hand, the lackluster response of the broader Jewish community tempered those feelings of joy, eliciting a prayer for the complete restoration.

Rabbi Yitzchak Etshalom[5] adds another dimension of interpretation of Psalm 126 by observing a connection with the Joseph narratives. The two passages are the only places in the entire Tanakh that use the term *alummah* (sheaf). When relating his first dream to his brothers, Joseph reports:

> There we were binding sheaves [*me'allemim alummim*] in the field, when suddenly my sheaf [*alummati*] stood up and re-

mained upright; then your sheaves [*alummotekhem*] gathered around and bowed low to my sheaf [*la-alummati*] (Genesis 37:7).

Similarly, Psalm 126 encourages those who tearfully work hard to plant because they will ultimately be rewarded with good crops:

> Though he goes along weeping, carrying the seed-bag, he shall come back with songs of joy, carrying his sheaves [*alummotav*] (Psalm 126:6).

Rabbi Etshalom observes that Joseph is the quintessential individual dreamer in Tanakh, and after much suffering, his dreams were realized. So too, says the psalmist, the nation of dreamers must look beyond its suffering and know that ultimately, redemption will arrive.

NOTES

1. At https://www.etzion.org.il/en/shiur15-psalm-121-i-will-lift-my-eyes-mountains-travelers-blessing; https://www.etzion.org.il/en/shiur-16-psalm-121-i-will-lift-my-eyes-mountains-travelers-blessing-continuation.
2. Alternatively, Ibn Ezra and Radak suggest that the psalmist looks "out there" for someone to help him, and realizes that only God can.
3. Elhanan Samet, *Iyyunim be-Mizmorei Tehillim* (Hebrew) (Tel Aviv: Yediot Aharonot, 2012), pp. 360–389.
4. See, for example, Job 42:10; Ezekiel 16:53–55.
5. Yitzchak Etshalom, "On Tears and Joy: A Study of Psalm 126" (Hebrew), *Megadim* 42 (2005), pp. 49–59.

Psalm 145:
Pure Praise

Because of its significance, we recite our beloved Psalm 145 (which makes up the majority of the *Ashrei* prayer) three times daily, which led Shelomo Goitein to dub it the "*Shema* of the Psalms."[1] It is the only psalm that begins with *tehillah*, "praise,"[2] and Amos Hakham suggests that perhaps the Sages named the book "*Tehillim*" after this psalm.[3]

In this essay, we consider different perspectives on this psalm as a chapter in Tanakh and then as part of our liturgy.

ALTERNATION BETWEEN CALL AND RESPONSE

Rabbi Avia Hacohen offers several ways of structuring the psalm.[4] The most convincing of these readings frames Psalm 145 as alternating between calls to praise and actual praise. The psalm would be set up as follows:

Call to praise:

> I will extol You, my God and king, and bless Your name forever and ever.
>
> Every day will I bless You and praise Your name forever and ever.

This essay is adapted from my article, "Perspectives on Psalm 145," in *The Keys to the Palace: Essays Exploring the Religious Value of Reading the Bible* (New York: Kodesh Press, 2017), pp. 259–275.

Praise:

> Great is the Lord and much acclaimed; His greatness cannot be fathomed.

Call to praise:

> One generation shall laud Your works to another and declare Your mighty acts.

> The glorious majesty of Your splendor and Your wondrous acts will I recite.

> Men shall talk of the might of Your awesome deeds, and I will recount Your greatness.

> They shall celebrate Your abundant goodness, and sing joyously of Your beneficence.

Praise:

> The Lord is gracious and compassionate, slow to anger and abounding in kindness.

> The Lord is good to all, and His mercy is upon all His works.

Call to praise:

> All Your works shall praise You, O Lord, and Your faithful ones shall bless You.

> They shall talk of the majesty of Your kingship, and speak of Your might,

> to make His mighty acts known among men and the majestic glory of His kingship.

Praise:

> Your kingship is an eternal kingship; Your dominion is for all generations.

> The Lord supports all who stumble, and makes all who are bent stand straight.

> The eyes of all look to You expectantly, and You give them their food when it is due.
>
> You give it openhandedly, feeding every creature to its heart's content.
>
> The Lord is beneficent in all His ways and faithful in all His works.
>
> The Lord is near to all who call Him, to all who call Him with sincerity.
>
> He fulfills the wishes of those who fear Him; He hears their cry and delivers them.
>
> The Lord watches over all who love Him, but all the wicked He will destroy.

Summary call:

> My mouth shall utter the praise of the Lord, and all creatures shall bless His holy name forever and ever.

In this structure, there is a growing trend of praise. The first round of praise is one verse, the second is two verses, and the third is eight verses. In the first call to praise, the psalmist refers to himself: "I will extol You...and [I] will bless...I bless You and [I] praise Your name forever and ever." The second call combines the psalmist as an individual with a group: "One generation shall laud...will I recite... men shall talk...I will recount...they shall celebrate." The third call is to the collective, rather than the individual: "All Your works shall praise You...Your faithful ones shall bless You...They shall talk... and speak." The psalm thus moves outward from the psalmist himself, to his joining the community in prayer, to then his focusing entirely on the community.

A similar progression occurs with the root *b-r-k*, "bless." In verses 1–2, the psalmist will bless God. In verse 10, the righteous bless God. Verse 21 expands to a longing that all people should bless God.[5] The psalm's final verse teaches that although individuals form a community through prayer, each individual retains his or her voice: "*My mouth shall utter*."[6]

The psalm's final verse also anticipates the day when "all creatures shall bless His holy name forever and ever." The individual at the beginning of the psalm will "bless Your name forever and ever," omitting "holy." God's name is referred to as "holy" with communal prayers, anticipating the concept of holy matters, *devarim she-bi-kedushah*, which require a quorum to praise God publicly (*Megillah* 23b). By coming together as a community, people have the power to sanctify God's name.

POTE'AH ET YADEKHA: YOU GIVE OPENHANDEDLY

> Rabbi Yosi [also] said: May my portion be of those who recite the entire *Hallel* every day. But that is not so, for a Master said: He who reads *Hallel* every day blasphemes and reproaches [the Divine Name]? We refer to the Verses of Song (*Pesukei de-Zimra*) (*Shabbat* 118b).[7]

Why would someone who recites the *Hallel* (Psalms 113–118) each day be considered a blasphemer? Rabbi Joseph Soloveitchik explains that Psalms 113–118 include praise for God's great miracles, including the exodus from Egypt and the crossing of the Jordan River in Joshua's time. We refer to this liturgy as *Hallel Mitzri*, the "Egyptian *Hallel*" (*Berakhot* 56a). We risk lessening the impact of God's acts if we equate all miracles – the daily and the supernatural. The daily recital of *Hallel*, then, would be a form of blasphemy. By treating it as a daily prayer, we would indicate that we no longer appreciate God's unusual acts as special. In contrast, Psalms 145–150 praise God for daily miracles, such as sustaining His creation and other natural phenomena.[8]

Similarly, the Talmud suggests that the optimal praises of God bless Him for the mundane:

> Rabbi Eleazar b. Avina says: Whoever recites [the psalm] "Praise of David" (Psalm 145) three times daily, is sure to inherit the world to come. What is the reason? Shall I say it is because

it has an alphabetical arrangement? Then let him recite, "Happy are they that are upright in the way" (Psalm 119), which has an eightfold alphabetical arrangement. Again, is it because it contains [the verse], "You open Your hand [*pote'ah et yadekha*]"? Then let him recite the great *Hallel* (Psalm 136), where it is written: "Who gives food to all flesh!" (Psalm 136:25). Rather, [the reason is] because it contains both (*Berakhot* 4b).

Replete with praise for God for the Creation and exodus, Psalm 136 receives honorable mention for its penultimate verse that praises God for day-to-day sustenance. Human nature revels in the supernatural and finds little to get excited about in the mundane. In contrast, Jewish thought gives primacy to the miracles of every day, rather than the extraordinary. The *Tur* explains that the verse *"pote'ah et yadekha"* is the primary reason that the Sages mandated reading Psalm 145 each day (*Orah Hayyim* 51). The *Shulhan Arukh* rules that if one does not have proper intention when reading this verse, he should return to recite it again (*Orah Hayyim* 51:7).

Rabbi Elhanan Samet[9] further observes similarities between Psalms 145 and 104:

Psalm 145	Psalm 104
15: The eyes of all look to You expectantly, and You give them their food when it is due (*enei kol elekha yesabberu, ve-attah noten lahem et okhlam be-itto*).	27: All of them look to You to give them their food when it is due (*kullam elekha yesabberun, la-tet okhlam be-itto*).
16: You give it openhandedly, feeding every creature to its heart's content (*pote'ah et yadekha u-masbia le-khol hai ratzon*).	28–29: Give it to them, they gather it up; open Your hand, they are well satisfied (*tiftah yadekha yisbe'un tov*); hide Your face, they are terrified; take away their breath, they perish and turn again into dust.

Both psalms stress the dependence of all creatures on God's sustenance. However, Psalm 104 notes that although God takes care of all creation, not every individual creature receives what it needs. Psalm 145, in contrast, is purely positive. God sustains all creatures without further qualification.

THE ACROSTIC AND THE MISSING *NUN*

Psalm 145 is an acrostic, illustrating a complete praise of God from the letters *aleph* to *tav*. Adele Berlin writes:

> The poet praises God with everything from A to Z; his praise is all-inclusive. More than that, the entire alphabet, the source of all words, is marshalled in praise of God. One cannot actually use all of the words in a language, but by using the alphabet one uses all potential words.[10]

The psalm also forms a literary inclusio that begins and ends with similar formulations. It begins with *tehillah*, a song of "praise," and ends *tehillat Hashem yedabber pi*, "my mouth shall utter the praise of the Lord." It begins *va-avarekha shimka le-olam va-ed*, "I will bless Your name forever and ever," and ends *vi-varekh kol basar shem kodsho le-olam va-ed*, "and all creatures shall bless His holy name forever and ever." Psalms that begin and end with the same wording are a sign of completeness, and the Talmud considers them to be special (*Berakhot* 9b–10a, cf. Tosafot s.v. *kol*). Another element of completeness in this psalm is its frequent use of the term *kol*, "all." The word *kol* appears seventeen times, including sixteen from verses 9–21. Adele Berlin suggests that this theme teaches that God does good to all, and therefore all should always praise Him.[11]

Psalm 145 contains verses beginning with each letter of the *aleph-bet* with the exception of *nun*. The Talmud offers a midrashic explanation which connects it to a verse in the book of Amos:

> Rabbi Johanan says: Why is there no *nun* in *Ashrei*? Because the fall of Israel's enemies [a euphemism for Israel] begins with it. For it is written: Fallen is the virgin of Israel, she shall rise

no more (Amos 5:2).... Rabbi Nahman b. Isaac says: Even so, David refers to it by inspiration and promises them an uplifting. For it is written: The Lord upholds all that fall (Psalm 145:14) (*Berakhot* 4b).

The Sages homiletically link Psalm 145 to Amos 5:2 to explain that although Amos prophesied that Israel shall rise no more, God raises *all* who fall – which would include Israel.

However, this is not a *peshat* explanation for the absence of the *nun*. Rather, the Talmud exploits the absence of a *nun* verse in Psalm 145 to address a difficulty with Amos 5:2. Radak and Meiri (on Psalm 145:1) state that we do not know the reason for the omission of the *nun*[12] and the talmudic passage interprets in the ways of *derash*. Some acrostics in the book of Psalms use the entire *aleph-bet*, whereas others – such as 25 and 34 – omit letters (*Ecclesiastes Rabbah* 1:13).[13] We do not know why some are complete while others are not.[14]

However, there is extra-biblical evidence that reflects the presence of a verse beginning with a *nun*. The discovery of the Dead Sea Scrolls (DSS) provided a Hebrew version of the verse: *Ne'eman Hashem bi-devarav ve-hasid be-khol ma'asav*, "The Lord is faithful in His words/deeds and gracious in all His works." Similarly, in the Septuagint (LXX), the Greek translation of Tanakh, there is a verse that reflects the reading *"ne'eman."*[15] It is possible that the original psalm omitted a verse beginning with *nun*. A later writer was troubled by that omission, and added this verse to complete the *aleph-bet*. From this vantage point, our Masoretic Text (MT) contains the original version. Alternatively, it is possible that the original psalm contained the verse beginning with *nun*, but a scribe accidentally omitted it. From this vantage point, the MT does not contain the original version and the LXX and DSS preserve the more authentic text.

Contemporary scholars debate which of these alternatives is more likely.[16] The best arguments in favor of the authenticity of the *nun* verse are: (1) It contains a new idea from the rest of the psalm. (2) The first blessing we recite after *haftarot* is "*ha-El ha-ne'eman be-khol devarav*," which is strikingly similar to the wording of this *nun* verse. Perhaps the formula of the blessing originates from this verse.[17]

The best arguments against the authenticity of the *nun* verse are: (1) other acrostics in the book of Psalms are also incomplete (e.g., 25, 34, 37), so the missing *nun* in 145 is not unusual. While true, however, this is not an argument against the *nun* as much as one demonstrating the plausibility of a missing letter in an acrostic. (2) The *nun* verse sounds suspiciously similar to *tzaddik Hashem be-khol derakhav ve-hasid be-khol ma'asav* (verse 17). This similarity may suggest that a later author copied a nearby verse in a feeble effort to supply a verse beginning with *nun*. However, there are other repetitions in the book of Psalms that serve as a chorus (e.g., 24:7, 9; 67:4, 6), so the near-repetition of a verse is plausible here as well. (3) It is more likely for a later writer or translator to smooth out a difficulty than for a scribe to accidentally omit a verse. (4) The Talmud already attests to the absence of a *nun* (*Berakhot* 4b), so this omission is ancient. Given that we recite the psalm regularly in our liturgy, an accidental omission of the *nun* becomes less likely. Overall, it appears more likely that the MT contains the original text, whereas the LXX and DSS reflect a later addition.

In his introduction to the book of Leviticus, Rabbi David Zvi Hoffmann addresses the general issue of variant texts. Although he grants the possibility of scribal errors in Tanakh, as a matter of religious policy we should not emend biblical texts, or it will open a Pandora's box that cannot be closed. It would be very difficult to learn Tanakh if we could never be certain about the authenticity of the text. Therefore, in practice we treat the MT as the original, even when we know of plausible variants.[18]

UNIVERSALISM AND PARTICULARISM IN PSALMS 145–150

The themes of universalism and particularism run throughout all Tanakh. Psalms 145–150, which comprise the heart of the morning *Pesukei de-Zimra*, reflect those two themes as well.[19] Psalm 145 is purely universalistic, as God sustains all creation. There is no special mention of the God-Israel relationship in this psalm.

In contrast, Psalms 146–149 contain elements of God's special relationship with Israel. Psalm 146 refers to God as the God of Jacob (146:5), and the concluding verse likewise mentions Israel: "The Lord shall reign forever, your God, O Zion, for all generations. Hallelujah" (146:10). Although the rest of the psalm applies to Jews and non-Jews alike, these verses add a distinctly Israelite element. While much of Psalm 147 praises God in nature, it also highlights the singular God-Israel relationship:

> The Lord rebuilds Jerusalem; He gathers in the exiles of Israel (147:2).

> He issued His commands to Jacob, His statutes and rules to Israel. He did not do so for any other nation; of such rules they know nothing. Hallelujah (147:19–20).

Psalm 148 resembles universalistic psalms such as 8 and 104, which praise God as the Creator of the cosmos. Its closing verse, however, stresses the God-Israel relationship: "He has exalted the horn of His people for the glory of all His faithful ones, Israel, the people close to Him. Hallelujah" (148:14). Psalm 149 contrasts Israel and her foes: "Let Israel rejoice in its maker; let the children of Zion exult in their king" (149:2). The psalm then focuses on God's future retribution against Israel's enemies.

Finally, Psalm 150 returns to universalism: "Let all that breathes praise the Lord. Hallelujah" (150:6). Thus, the bookends of these six psalms are universalistic, whereas the middle four psalms contain more particularistic elements, as well.[20]

PSALM 145 AS LITURGY

The Talmud (*Berakhot* 4b) teaches that "whoever recites [the psalm] Praise of David three times daily is sure to inherit the world to come." Amos Hakham[21] notes that our printed text is not the original talmudic text. The original passage read, "whoever recites [the psalm] Praise of David daily." Rabbi Amram Gaon had the original version in his Siddur (c. 875 CE). In the Geonic period, the practice developed to recite this psalm three times daily to increase the likelihood of saying it at least once (*Shibbolei ha-Leket* 7). Evidently, this new practice crept into the text of the Talmud. The daily practice reflects the psalm's second verse, *be-khol yom avarakheka*, "every day will I bless You." The second half of the verse reads, *va-ahalelah shimkha le-olam va-ed*, "I will praise Your name forever and ever." Although the plain sense of forever and ever would mean "for the rest of my life," the Sages understand the verse as referring literally to forever, requiring continued praise into the afterlife. Hence, praising God every day leads to a share in the world to come.

In addition to the complete sense of praise that the psalm exhibits with its acrostic and inclusio, our tradition to append verses at the beginning and end of the psalm adds a new dimension of completion. Prior to the psalm, we open with the verses in Psalm 84:5 and 144:15, which both begin with the word "*ashrei*." At the conclusion of the psalm, we add 115:18, which ends in "Hallelujah." In the liturgical form that we recite it, Psalm 145 now begins with the first word of the book of Psalms, and ends with the final word in the book of Psalms. By reading Psalm 145, then, we symbolically read the entire book.

Additionally, by adding the verses at the beginning and end of the psalm, we shift the universalistic psalm to a more Israel-centered focus: "Happy the people who have it so; happy the people whose God is the Lord" (144:15) prefaces Psalm 145 with Israel's joy in serving God. The psalm concludes by expressing a longing for all humanity to serve God: "all creatures shall bless His holy name forever and ever" (145:21). We follow that with an expression that we currently do so: "But we will bless the Lord now and forever. Hallelujah" (115:18).[22] Finally, Rabbi Amram Gaon explained that adding 115:18 to the end of Psalm 145 has it conclude with "Hallelujah" in order to connect it to the following five psalms of *Pesukei de-Zimra*, which begin and end with "Hallelujah" (quoted in *Tur, Orah Hayyim* 51).[23]

The array of perspectives on this beloved psalm is not surprising. Its love of God and its ability to move the individual into a growing community of worshippers who accept God's kingship have indeed made it into the "*Shema* of the psalms."

NOTES

1. Shelomo D. Goitein, *Biblical Studies* (Hebrew) (Tel Aviv: Yavneh, 1957), p. 228. Several medieval commentators identified what they believed to be the most important psalm: Ibn Ezra selected Psalm 139 based on its philosophical themes. Radak preferred Psalm 1. Rabbi Yosef Hayyun considered Psalm 145 to be the most exalted.
2. In contrast, fifty-seven psalms contain the word *mizmor* in their opening verses.
3. Amos Hakham, *Da'at Mikra: Psalms* vol. 2 (Hebrew) (Jerusalem: Mosad HaRav Kook, 1979), p. 570, n. 2. See also II Chronicles 29:30, where Hezekiah commands the priests and Levites *le-hallel la-Hashem be-divrei David ve-Asaf ha-hozeh*, to praise the Lord in the words of David and Asaph the seer. Cf. Ezra 3:10; Nehemiah 12:24, which also use the term *le-hallel* regarding the usage of David's prayers. These verses suggest that the name for book of *Tehillim* already was developing in the late biblical period.
4. Avia Hacohen, *Tefillah le-El Hai: The Journey of the Soul and the Spirit of the Song in the Book of Psalms* (Hebrew) (En Tzurim: Yeshivat HaKibbutz HaDati, 2007), pp. 93–111.
5. Nahum M. Sarna et al. (*Olam HaTanakh: Psalms* vol. 2 [Hebrew] [Tel Aviv: Dodson-Iti, 1999], p. 267) observes that Psalms 146–150 present the community praising God rather than the individual, and suggests that one may view Psalms 145–150 as a unit where the individual calls on others to praise God in chapter 145, and the following five psalms respond to that call.
6. Cf. Binyamin Gezundheit and Reuven Kimelman, "A Praise of David: Structure and Meaning" (Hebrew), *Megadim* 49 (2008), pp. 61–62. A similar progression from the individual to the community occurs in Psalm 103, and that psalm also concludes with the voice of the individual still present.
7. Rashi understands the *Pesukei de-Zimra* as referring specifically to Psalms 148 and 150, which feature the word *hallelu*. Most others understand this passage as referring to all of Psalms 145–150, which are recited in the daily liturgy (Rif; Rambam *Hilkhot Tefillah* 7:12; *Soferim* 18:1). Halakhah codifies the recitation of Psalms 145–150 as the "daily *Hallel*" but if someone comes late to services and does not have time to recite them all, we follow Rashi in giving priority to chapters 148 and 150 (*Shulhan Arukh, Orah Hayyim* 52:1).
8. Arnold Lustiger, *Derashot HaRav: Selected Lectures of Rabbi Joseph B. Soloveitchik* (Union City, NJ: Ohr, 2003), pp. 153–156.
9. Elhanan Samet, at http://vbm-torah.org/archive/tehillim70/51tehillim.htm.
10. Adele Berlin, "The Rhetoric of Psalm 145," in *Biblical and Related Studies*

Presented to Samuel Iwry, ed. Ann Kort and Scott Morschauser (Winona Lake, IN: Eisenbrauns, 1985), p. 18.
11. Ibid., p. 19.
12. Uriel Simon (*Four Approaches to the Book of Psalms: from Saadiah Gaon to Abraham ibn Ezra*, trans. Lenn. J. Schramm [New York: SUNY Press, 1991], p. 104, n. 45) quotes the tenth-century Karaite Yefet ben Ali, who speculated that the omission of the *nun* verse suggests that it is impossible to fully praise God. Although it is a nice idea homiletically, there are acrostics in the book of Psalms (111, 112, and 119) that do complete the *aleph-bet*, so Yefet's explanation is inadequate at the level of *peshat*.
13. Gezundheit and Kimelman ("A Praise of David," p. 64, n. 19) quote Yaakov Bazak, who observes that the acrostics ascribed to David (25, 34, 37, 145) omit letters whereas those not ascribed to David (111, 112, 119) have complete *aleph-bet* acrostics.
14. For further discussion, see Ronald Benun, "Evil and the Disruption of Order: A Structural Analysis of the Acrostics in the First Book of Psalms," *Journal of Hebrew Scriptures* 6:5 (2006).
15. The Greek reflects the reading, "*Ne'eman Elokim be-khol devarav ve-hasid be-khol ma'asav.*"
16. See Sarna et al., *Olam ha-Tanakh: Psalms* vol. 2, pp. 268–269, for a summary of both sides of the argument.
17. Reuven Kimelman ("Psalm 145: Theme, Structure, and Impact," *Journal of Biblical Literature* 113 [1994], p. 50) argues that a later writer drew from the blessing of the *haftarah* and added it to the text of the psalm, rather than the reverse.
18. For a broader discussion of traditional sources pertaining to text variants in Tanakh, see Amnon Bazak, *Ad ha-Yom ha-Zeh: Until This Day: Fundamental Questions in Bible Teaching* (Hebrew), ed. Yoshi Farajun (Tel Aviv: Yediot Aharonot, 2013), pp. 183–243.
19. See also Sarna et al., *Olam ha-Tanakh: Psalms* vol. 2, p. 267.
20. For further analysis of the interrelationship between Psalms 145–150, see Binyamin Gezundheit, "*Pesukei de-Zimra*: A Literary and Conceptual Unit Based on Contextual Interpretation" (Hebrew), *Megadim* 54 (2013), pp. 85–109.
21. Hakham, *Da'at Mikra: Psalms* vol. 2, p. 579. Cf. Rabbi Akiva Eiger (*Gilyon ha-Shas* on *Berakhot* 4b), who notes that Rosh, Tur, and Roke'ah likewise did not have "three times" in their versions.
22. Cf. Hakham, *Da'at Mikra*, p. 580; Gezundheit and Kimelman, "A Praise of David," p. 68.
23. For a conceptual approach to the additional verses, see Rabbi Joseph B. Soloveitchik, *Al ha-Tefillah* (Hebrew), ed. Reuven Grodner (New York: OU Press, 2012), pp. 27–39.